I0560462

Praise for Pilgrim Paths to Assisi

The tale truly takes the reader on a spiritual journey. This work ... is, in many respects, a love story, engagingly describing the author's quest to fulfill his dreams about learning, in as many senses as possible, the ways of the remarkable man who taught simple, truthful lessons and experienced a particularly deep connection to God.

-U.S Review of Books

For thousands of years, humans have been trying to define the meaning of life. Not unlike Francis or Homer, Russ has found a way to describe something of far more value: The meaning of the journey. This book is a treasure. Whether you are a seasoned trekker like me or an armchair traveler, you can find some wonderful stories that might get you out on your own pilgrimage to Spain or Italy someday. This book is an excellent reminder that it is never too late to set out, one step at a time, on a grand adventure that can define a well-lived life.

—Christopher Hurst, *Climbing Mount Kilimanjaro*

Reading Pilgrim Paths to Assisi, the Way of Saint Francis comes alive

—Matt Harms, Author of *The Way of St. Francis* and other pilgrimage guidebooks

GOOD MORNING, GOOD PEOPLE!

Stories for the Way of St. Francis

RUSS EANES

The Walker Press

The Walker Press

www.thewalkerpress.com

Copyright © 2025 by Russ Eanes

All rights reserved.

No part of this book may be reproduced in any form or by any electronic or mechanical means, including information storage and retrieval systems, without written permission from the author, except for the use of brief quotations in a book review.

ISBN softcover: 979-8-9910673-2-4

ISBN ebook: 979-8-9910673-3-1

All photos are by the author

Cover design by Andre Eanes

Cover image from stain glass in the church of San Damiano, Assisi

Contact the author at russeanes.com

To the Pilgrim Community: you have become my friends, brothers, sisters and family.

Also by Russ Eanes

The Walk of a Lifetime: 500 Miles on the Camino de Santiago

Pilgrim Paths to Assisi: 300 Miles on the Way of St. Francis

Contents

Italy

Florence

Assisi

Rome

The Way of St. Francis

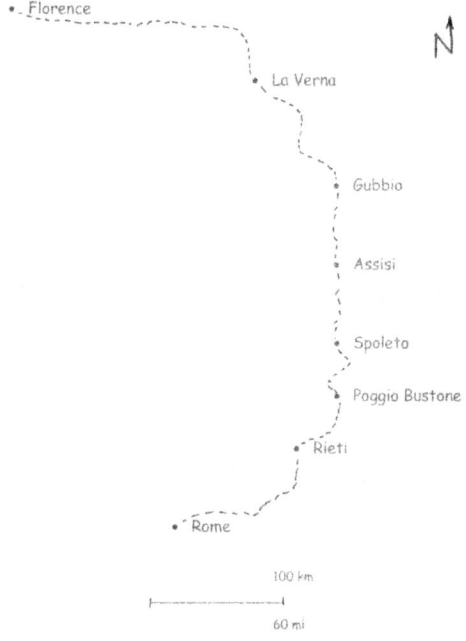

Author's Note

Writing a book about places and people from Italy is always a challenge when it comes to spelling. Which to use? Italian? English? In this book, I have used both.

Italian places have their Italian names, especially churches. When it comes to people, I have used both. If the English version is more familiar to speakers of English (such as Francis vs. Francesco) I have used it. If the Italian name is more familiar (such as Bernardo vs. Bernard) I have used it. For those who would insist on it being one way, or the other, I beg your forgiveness.

Lastly, in Italy, a monastery is a convent, so I use that term.

Introduction

Good Morning, Good People is born out of a love for
history's most beloved saint, Francis of Assisi. Even
though he died nearly 800 years ago, Francis has been a
companion for my entire adult life. I'm not a Franciscan
in any formal sense—I'm not even Catholic—but his life
has informed and influenced me as I have wrestled with
what it means to consider oneself a follower of Christ in
the modern, post-Christian age. His love of God and his
fellow human beings, his reverence for animals and the
natural world and his life of simplicity all have resonated
with me from the first time I read about him. His
mystical nature appealed to my own mystical bent.

Alongside Jesus, Moses, Mohammed, and Buddha,
Francis is one of the world's most widely known,
beloved, and revered religious figures. According to
contemporary Franciscan speaker and author Richard
Rohr, "When Pope John Paul II wanted to gather the
leaders of all the world religions to have a respectful
interfaith dialogue in the 1980s, the only city in the

world that they could agree to meet in was Assisi,
because the memory of St. Francis does not carry any
negative baggage, even to other religions."[1] Books about
his life and references about him in books proliferate.
Apparently, he has the longest card catalog entry of any
person in the Library of Congress.[2] In Italian he's *Il
Poverello*, "The Little Poor Man," and he's the patron
saint of Italy, along with Catherine of Sienna.
According to Angela Maria Serrachioli, "Francis is in
the DNA of Italians just as James is in that of the
Spanish…"[3]

Since 1986 he has also been the patron saint of the
worldwide ecological movement. In an age of disbelief,
skepticism, evangelical fervor, and religious extremism,
his wide acceptance comes as a welcome relief. In an
age of overconsumption that is heating an already
ecologically threatened planet, his life of simplicity and
care for the natural world points to hope. The recently
deceased Pope—eager to emphasize his own commitment to the poor of the world—even became history's
first Pope Francis.

More than a dozen years ago I learned that there
was a new pilgrimage route in Italy—The Way of Saint
Francis, now more than 550 kilometers in length—
which walks an ancient landscape that still breathes of
him. Since 2019 I have repeatedly walked parts of the
Way of St. Francis, which traverses the mountains of
central Italy between Florence in Rome, with Assisi as its
midway point. I have walked it alone, with my wife and
with groups, and each time I am struck by how deeply
spiritual it is. My hope in writing this book is to inspire

pilgrims to not just walk and appreciate the beauty of this trail, but to understand and learn from Francis as they traverse his beloved countryside. Walking his countryside, his life speaks for our time as powerfully as it did his. And there is no better way to experience it than on foot (as he did) feeling the gentle breezes through the olive groves, seeing the waves of red poppies as they shimmer in the fields, or the sun as it sets from the hilltop towns that seem to be carved out of the sheer rock.

Francis, as an Italian mountain guide told me, was more than anything a pilgrim, a person always on the move, animated by a spirit from God, who loved the world and wanted to experience it all. For this reason, perhaps more than any other pilgrimage, the Way of St. Francis lends itself to stories.

Out of my first three journeys, a book emerged, *Pilgrim Paths to Assisi: 300 Miles on the Way of St. Francis,* a chronicle of walking the entire route. Because of that book, beginning in 2023, I have hosted groups on this route and shared the life and legends of Francis along the way. This book is a collection of those stories and more, all based on some very old collections of legends about the life of Francis.

I am not a scholar or historian, but a writer, and while I have done considerable reading and research, this book is in no way exhaustive. It is not a biography. Scores of biographies have been written about him— and I have read most of the recent and best ones—but they do not always agree with the chronology, dates or actual details of certain events in his life. In this book I have leaned heavily on one: *Francis of Assisi: A Revolutionary Life*, by Adrian House. His affectionate, detailed and occasionally conjectural telling of his life is my favorite, and since the framework of this book is largely chronological, I have followed House's chronology. Not all of the stories in this book took place along the Way of St. Francis, but I included them to give a more complete picture of his life and character.

I have tried as much as possible to tease out and synthesize the *facts* of Francis' life as well as his spirit. I try not to pass judgment on the historicity or facts of the stories, but simply let them speak for themselves; sometimes a work of fiction can be just as "true," as one based on fact. My desire is to get to the essence of what the story can teach us. When you add this to the physical location of the stories, they come alive and stay in our memory.

Many of the legends were written down decades after his death and they were written for particular purposes, often slanted to satisfy the needs of their authors. Dates are almost nonexistent in the tales and all of the best collections are thematic rather than chronological. Of those collections of legends, I have leaned mostly on three: *The Little Flowers of Saint Francis* (Anonymous author,14th century); *We Were With St. Francis* (a collection of stories from before 1250, based on a Latin manuscript commonly called *The Legends of Perugia);* and *Legends of the Three Companions* (also written before 1250.) Last two collections probably come from the same source and were told by Leo, Ruffino and Angelo, the three companions who were with him nearly

continually in the last years of his life. They came from
a time, just decades after Francis' death, when the Franciscan Order was in danger of losing the original
charism of its founder.

There is more on each of these and other sources in
the Appendix and Bibliography. At the end the reader
can find a timeline of Francis' life, along with that of
Clare of Assisi.

While anyone can enjoy what I have written, this
small book is intended primarily for pilgrims, so, in addition to the stories, I have added some additional information about some of the places that the stories
occurred, some of which you might not even find in a
guidebook. There is a location index in the back that
cross-indexes geographic locations with the stories, so
that pilgrims can find stories that took place in certain
towns.

In addition, I have added a few details about some
of the other people, including saints, who are connected
to St. Francis and whose stories also take place along
the way.

The country I live in is currently in political, social and
economic upheaval and crisi; a materialistic, fragmented
and secular-dominated culture that is paradoxically spiritually starved and searching for authentic and deep
spirituality. In that sense, it is not all that different from
the time of Francis. I hope that these stories, combined
(hopefully) with a walk on the Way of Saint Francis can

inject some hope into our time. Writing them has certainly helped me. Seracchioli, who originally conceived of and then marked out much of the Way of Saint Francis said it well:

> Here it is not a matter of creating an alternative to one of the 'major pilgrimages' from nothing, but of walking with the same pilgrim spirit in the midst of a nature in all its beauty, stopping and staying in places full of history and Spirit, following a route that cannot be chronological but that takes you to the locations where the fundamental episodes of the life of the 'perfect pilgrim' took place[4]

PART I

A Movement Begins

Early Life of Francis

GIOVANNI BERNADONE, known to us in history as Saint Francis, was born in Assisi in 1181 or 1182. He died there 44 years later, a life short by modern standards but outsized in its impact on his own time and on history. He lived more in those four decades than many live in a life twice as long.

Francis's father, Pietro Bernadone, was a wealthy cloth merchant among the emerging middle classes of Umbria in central Italy. Umbria, and Assisi in particular, was also central in the political struggles of the time. The major political powers for nearly 400 years had been the Holy Roman Emperor, whose realm included much of Northern Italy, and the Pope, who ruled a patchwork of states in central Italy much like a secular ruler. In Francis' time, Emperor Frederick II, of German descent, was born and raised in the castle or *Rocca* above Assisi.

His mother, Pica, was possibly French, or at least knew French, and called her son Francesco (Francis in

English), meaning "little Frenchy," and the nickname stuck. Pietro took his son on journeys to France and Belgium where he traded for the latest in fabrics. Along the way the young Francesco would have learned the romantic tales and songs of medieval troubadours, legends of courtly love and valiant knights. They remained with him during his life, the poetry and music influencing his preaching. He was sometimes known as "God's Troubadour," because he imitated troubadours in his manner of preaching. His own poem, *Canticle of the Sun,* also set to music, is credited as being the first poem written in Italian (versus Latin).

The young Francis received an education and enjoyed the privileges associated with being the son of wealth. He caroused with the sons of other affluent merchants and nobility, sponsoring drinking parties and earning a reputation as a bit of a playboy. During his later teenage years Assisi declared itself an independent commune, rebelling against the representatives of the Holy Roman Emperor who had occupied the *Rocca*. The townspeople attacked the castle and tore it down. Many of its stones may have been used to build a new set of walls around the city and Francis may have learned stone masonry during this time. In addition to the emperor, they also drove out most nobility of the town who owned large, fortified houses and also owned much of the land around the city. These nobles fled to nearby Perugia and itched for a fight to regain their lost lands.

Like many other young men of his age, Francis longed for the glories of warfare. The conflict with Perugia would provide that opportunity. To win his reputation he went with several of his fellows to battle with neighboring Perugia, outfitted in an expensive suit of armor. But he was to win neither riches nor glory; he was captured during the brief battle of Collestrada, which ended in a humiliating defeat for Assisi. He suffered for at least two years in a damp and cold prison, while peace was negotiated, and ransom was raised for his release.

Francis came home a changed man. His time in captivity had been both physically, mentally and spiritually trying. The dank dungeon where he was held captive was conducive to disease. Always frail, he likely contracted tuberculosis while he was there and returned home sick, spending much of the next year being nursed back to health. He would be plagued throughout the rest of his life with bouts of sickness.

Once the center of a group of carousing young men, he no longer felt drawn to his formerly hedonistic lifestyle. He was said to be more serious. Working in his father's business did not interest him. Not quite yet ready to give up the idea of earning honor and glory as a knight, he joined a local nobleman—Count Gentile—on his way to join Walter de Brienne, who was gathering a force in southeast Italy to depart for the Holy Land, part of the Fourth Crusade.

Once again, he adorned himself in armor and splendid clothing and set out in flourish and fanfare. He got no farther than Spoleto, about 30 miles south, when he was overtaken by a bout of malaria and was taken to bed with a fever. In delirium he had a dream where a voice told him to return to home, where, "he would be told what to do." He abandoned the quest (perhaps to the relief of his traveling companions) and returned to Assisi.

A period of aimlessness set in. At times drawn to the carousing of his companions, he also became moody and depressed. He took to wandering the countryside on horseback. One day he passed near a Lazar house—a place of refuge for lepers—a few miles below Assisi. He'd had a lifetime revulsion for lepers, but he recounted later that in a spontaneous act he dismounted and kissed the leper and gave him money. The leper gave him a blessing. Returning home he took some of his father's money and returned with it to the lazar house. He said that this act of kissing the leper and the resultant donation of money was his turning point and he felt drawn from then on to assist the needy and outcast from society, the numbers of which he would soon join. He felt like a completely different person inside.

As he pondered his future, he took solace in solitude. He wandered the wooded mountainside of Mt. Subasio, south of Assisi, where he sought the solitude of caves. Sometimes he was accompanied by friends (Angelo di Tancredi may have been one) where he would wander off alone to pray.

Another place he favored was the small, decaying church of San Damiano, about a kilometer below Assisi. While sitting in the ruin one day, he gazed up at a painted crucifix hanging above the altar where he heard the voice of Christ say, "Rebuild my church." Whereas the mission to the lepers had given him a new sense of identity, this voice gave him a concrete, visible mission.

He now had a calling and a purpose in life.

YOU CAN VISIT several of these early, important places of Assisi when you walk the pilgrimage route. San Damiano, less than a kilometer below the town still has the atmosphere of Francis and Clare and is one of my favorite places in the environs of the city. About four kilometers' walk south of Assisi, on the side of Mt. Subasio is the Eremo di Carcieri, which became a Franciscan Hermitage in Francis' life, built around the caves that he frequented before and after his call by God.

2

A break with his family

AFTER HEARING the voice of Christ from the crucifix, Francis left the ruin of San Damiano and soon encountered a country priest who was responsible for the ruined church. Francis gave him the coins he was carrying at the time and hurried home for more.

He would need much more money to restore the church and rebuild its crumbling roof, so over the next weeks he secretly took bolts of cloth from his father's storehouse and rode to the nearby town of Foligno, where he sold them. He returned to the priest and gave him the money, in particular asking him to keep the oil lamp lit on the altar. He began working on the restoration of the church.

Pietro soon realized what Francis had done, and in anger locked him in a cellar in his own house, before setting out on one of his annual trade journeys to France. Francis was humiliated and shamed but remained steadfast. Before long, his mother felt sorry for him and realizing his determination, took pity on him and let him free. He returned to San Damiano and resumed his work.

His father's return from France brought things to a head. Seeing his son free, he went and found him at work again on San Damiano. Embarrassed and humiliated by Francis's behavior, in a fit of rage he hauled him back to town to face the ruling consuls. In his time, a father had the right to not only to disown, but to banish a son from the town. The local consuls, sensing this might be more a religious matter than secular law, and happy to defer the matter to another authority, referred Pietro to Bishop Guido. Pietro was undeterred and dragged him to the bishop's palace where he demanded justice and the drama reached its peak.

Guido was not totally surprised by the encounter. Francis had come to him on many occasions and Guido was familiar with his spiritual longings and had tried to counsel him. He knew that Francis had been taking his father's goods and selling them, and the priest to whom Francis had given money had in fact brought it to him, afraid to handle money that he knew was raised by the theft of his father's cloth.

Pietro demanded the money that Francis had given the priest, now in the bishop's possession, as he sought to publicly and officially disown Francis. Before his father could complete his case, Francis disappeared through a side door into the bishop's palace and disrobed. Clutching his clothes in his arms, with the bag of coins on top, he returned naked to the bishop's courtyard, and in front of all those assembled he handed the clothes and money to his father, saying, "I give these back to you. From now on I have one father, the Father in Heaven."

Bishop Guido, either in a gesture of modesty or in a symbol of the protection of the church, removed his own robe and placed it over the young man. Francis's father was speechless; his mother was in tears. Still furious, Pietro received the clothes and money, and then he and grief-stricken Pica disappeared from the scene, and from the historical record.

The matter settled, Francis was given the tunic and trousers of a peasant and allowed to go free, as carried away by the event as he was the creator of it.

TODAY THE PLACE in Assisi where Francis was confronted by his father is marked by a statue that stands in the middle of this courtyard, next to the Santuario della Spogliazione, or "Room of the Stripping." Nearby you can also visit the family home and see the cellar room where his father imprisoned him. In front of it is a bronze sculpture of his two parents, his mother standing with a broken chain in her hands, signifying Francis' break with his family.

In the central piazza of Foligno, south of Spello along the pilgrimage route there is a plaque and sculpture that memorializes the sale of his father's cloth to raise money for the rebuilding of San Damiano

3

North to Gubbio

REJECTED by Assisi and clothed in a simple peasant's tunic, Francis was now free, but not certain yet about his next steps. He certainly had no clue about his calling from God, other than the vocation to rebuild a crumbling country church. Thinking it best to change his environ, and wanting the comfort of a friend, he wandered north to Gubbio. He was now 24 or 25 years old.

With each step northward. Francis felt increasingly liberated: he no longer had to hide what he was doing, steal from his father, or worry about his reputation. His inner spirit now in tune with God, he became exuberant, like a young man in love. He didn't have yet a name for her, but he embraced this new love: Lady Poverty. Like the troubadours he had met on journeys with his father to France, he sang songs of love to this Lady.

Gubbio was 20 miles to the north through the Valley of the Chiasco river, and the home of an old friend from his boyhood, Giacomello Spadalunga, also the wealthy son of a cloth merchant. The two were likely imprisoned together in Perugia, after the battle of Collestrada and Francis knew that he was someone who he could trust. According to the legends, it was winter or early spring when he set out on his journey.

He had not gotten far before he ran into trouble. In his simple dress, singing in French like a troubadour, he was set upon by a band of robbers. Asking him who he was, and where he was going, he replied, "I am herald of the Great King. What's that to you?" They demanded money from him, and he replied that he had none. Searching him, and thinking him mad or a fool, they stripped him of his simple garment and threw him naked into a ditch filled with snow.

Bruised and cold, yet undeterred, he sought refuge in a nearby Benedictine monastery, Santa Maria di Valfabbrica. He rang the bell at the gate, standing naked in the cold. The monks were shocked when they encountered him and also assumed that he was a madman. After throwing a cloak over him, they fed him scraps of food and forced him to work in the kitchen. He stayed with them for a few days, before they sent him on his way. He arrived in Gubbio at his friend Giacomello's home, hungry, nearly naked, and penniless.

Giacomello was likely startled to see his friend in this state, but still welcomed Francis warmly, giving him food and lodging and new clothing—a hermit's garb, consisting of a tunic and belt along with sandals and a staff. The tradition of hospitality and charity that began on that first visit must have been profound, because eventually the Spadalunga warehouse became a monastery. Next to it arose the spacious Basilica di San Francesco, a beautiful structure, now with a statue of Francis and a wolf out in front.

CHIESA SANTA MARIA ASSUNTA and the old Benedictine Convent by the same name are in Valfabbrica and can be visited when you are walking the Way.

Also along this route is the Convent of San Pietro in Vignetto, already an established benedictine monastery in Francis' time and a wonderful place to stay today, as the confraternity of St. James continues the ministry of hospitality in the way of the medieval pilgrims. I find it to be one of the most peaceful places along the entire pilgrimage route.

The Chiesa di Caprignone, near San Pietro in Vignetto, was the scene of a large and important Chapter of the Franciscans in 1217. You will pass it along the way, though unfortunately I have never encountered it open.

The Chiesa San Francesco in Gubbio is one of my favorite churches along the pilgrimage route with beautiful and even mystical frescoes by Ottaviano Nelli, some of my favorites along the Way. This ancient church was constructed in 1255 on the lands of the Spadalunga family and was part of a vast Franciscan convent, all given in honor of Francis, whom Gubbio had adopted and with whom he had a close relationship.

Cheerful builder

HIS TIME in Gubbio relieved the immediate pressure that he had been under in Assisi, but Francis knew that his mission was back at San Damiano, so after a brief stay in Gubbio, returned to his hometown. In obedience to the voice from the Crucifix: he would rebuild the church.

To feed himself, Francis begged his food. To obtain building materials, he begged stones. He must have appeared a fool, this slightly built son of a wealthy merchant, wandering the streets of his hometown barefoot and needy. The locals jeered at him, pelting him with stones and mud. Ridicule from his fellow townspeople did not deter him; stripped of even his pride, he felt freer than ever. (The local derision did not last long; within 10 years he was welcome and revered by Assisi, though never, apparently, by his family.)

Francis continued to go to mass at Santa Maria Maggiore, and there he heard the gospel reading one day:

Preach as you go, saying, "the Kingdom of heaven is at hand." Heal the sick... cleanse lepers, cast out demons... give without pay. Take no gold, nor silver, nor copper in your belts, no bag for your journey, nor two tunics, nor sandals, nor a staff... as you enter a house, salute it. And if the house is worthy, let your peace come upon it.[1]

This gospel passage sharpened Francis' calling; he would become like Christ in poverty. He also began a practice that he would continue throughout his life (and which he would encode into his Rule) of giving the greeting of the Peace of God, whenever he entered a home.

Francis also added preaching to his task of rebuilding and in addition took time to visit the lepers who lived outside of the city, at a place called Rivotorto. At first, he worked alone, but in spite of the humiliating treatment, his preaching and his genuine faith was having an effect on the town, in particular some of his former friends. Francis had been a popular young man before his conversion and some of his closest friends had not forgotten him. Thus began a further scandal, as one after another of these young men—the cream of society —turned their back on privilege and joined Francis.

The first to join him, however, was not one of those young friends, but Bernardo di Quintavalle, a rich and highly respected notary who frequently invited Francis to his house to talk. One night their conversation went late, and Francis, to avoid making a show of his piety, begged to go to bed and feigned sleep. After some time, thinking Bernardo asleep, he quietly woke to say his prayers. But Bernardo was also feigning sleep; when he saw Francis on his knees—thinking no one was watching him—he became convinced that what Francis had been preaching to him was true. The next morning he told Francis that he no longer needed his wealth, that he wanted to give it all away to follow him.

A legend records that at the same time Bernardo had decided to join Francis, a third young man, Peter of Catanio, a young lawyer from Assisi, also decided to join them, and then there were three.

WHEN YOU ARE in Assisi or other Umbrian towns you will notice the wide variety of building materials that have been used and reused over the years, from Roman brick to Umbrian limestone of pink, brown and white. The tradition there of building and rebuilding with the local stone has been going on for over a thousand years. I love to touch the stones of San Damiano, the best-preserved of all the Franciscan sites in the city, imagining that Francis himself had laid them in their place.

5

The Brothers discover their vocation

WHEN THE FIRST BROTHERS, Bernardo and Peter of Catanio, had only just agreed to follow him, the two of them, along with Francis, sought to know their vocation. Francis had never planned to live the life of a hermit and, frankly, had not known exactly *how* he was supposed to live. He just followed the path that he felt God, along with Lady Poverty, had laid out for him.

As Francis said at the end of his life, in his *Testament*

> After the Lord had given me brothers, no one showed me what I was to do, but the Most High himself revealed that I should live according to the pattern of the holy gospel

The three entered San Nicolas church, on the northern edge of the Piazza del Commune and approached the book of the Gospels, praying for guidance, then opening it three times, randomly, confident that the message revealed to them was from God.

The first reading was from Matthew 19:21: "If you wish to be perfect, go, sell what you have and give it to the poor and you shall have treasure in heaven."

The second was from Luke 9:3: "Take nothing for your journey"

The third and last was from Matt 16:24: "If any man will come after me, let him deny himself."

In the 13th century, individuals did not have access to the scriptures in their vernacular, let alone possess their own Bibles. The book they opened was a *missal,* a book of readings used for saying mass, and its text would have been in Latin. Francis, schooled early in his life, was able to read and translate the three texts.

What stands out, however, is the parallel meaning in each text: Christ was asking him and his companions to renounce their worldly goods and follow him. According to the legends, as soon as they left the church, Bernardo and Peter, "kicked off their shoes and exchanged their clothes for a habit tied at the waist with a rope."*

As Bernardo was giving away the proceeds from the sale of his property, Francis was approached by Silvester, an elderly priest from whom Francis had begged stones. He had a reputation for being avaricious, and complaining that Francis had not paid him enough for the stones, demanded some of the coins. Legends say that Francis thrust his hand into Berardo's pocket and gave Silvester a handful of coins, a gesture so disarming

---

* This missal is still in existence and in the possession of the Walters Art Museum of Baltimore, and is considered a valuable relic, since St. Francis touched it.

that it converted him, and he also soon decided to join Francis' small band, as the fourth brother.

With the help from his new brothers, San Damiano and another church, San Pietro, were rebuilt and they turned their attention to another dilapidated structure, the tiny church Santa Maria degli Angeli, near the cross-roads between Assisi and Perugia. This small church, which with its surrounding property was known as the Porziuncola, or "little portion." It was owned by the Benedictine monks at San Benedetto, on the slopes of Mt. Subasio, south of Assisi, who agreed to allow them the perpetual use of the land for the annual price of a basket of fish. After they restored the church, the brothers built some small huts in the clearing and set about to minister to lepers, to help with the harvests in the fields and to beg for their food.

A young man, Giles, from a local peasant family, had seen them giving away Bernardo's coins near San Giorgio and he came down to the Porziuncola to find Francis and the others. After declaring his intention to join them, Francis quickly tested his resolve and ordered him to give his cloak to a beggar who had arrived at the same time, in search of alms. Giles handed it over without hesitation and became the fifth brother to join their band.

In the next months, several more joined. Among them: Sabbatino, a scholar who would accompany Francis to Egypt; Morico, a Cruciger knight who met Francis while he was working in a leper house; John of Capella, known later for his misguided zeal. Rounding out their numbers were Bernard of Viridente, Barbaro, and Philip (known as "the long"). The seventh, and last, was a brother of particular significance: Angelo di Tancredi, among the oldest of Francis' friends, a nobleman and son of a consul of Assisi, for whom renouncing the world, his wealth and his title was a more costly decision than Francis'. But once he joined, he became one of Francis' closest companions and it ought to be noted that he is one of the four brothers buried around him in his tomb.*

With them, a movement was born, and it is no coincidence that they numbered 12.

JUST BELOW THE main piazza in Assisi are the remains of San Nicolas, entered via the Underground Assisi Museum. The museum is at the level of the original Roman Forum and is worth a visit. A self-guided tour will take the visitor around an area that is now underneath the current piazza above.

---

* It is believed that Angelo was the source for information about the early life of Francis and was probably one of his companions when he wandered the hills and caves of Mt. Subasio, years before.

6

Good morning, Good People

EVEN AFTER THE brothers had discovered what they thought was their vocation, they still had an uneasy relationship with Assisi, their hometown. Taking a vow of poverty had been difficult enough for Francis; now the group of young men following him made that even harder to swallow. As Jesus said, "A prophet is not without honor, except in his hometown."

To quote Francis:

> …beloved brothers, God and his mercy has chosen us not only for our salvation but also to save many souls. Let us go throughout the world and, by our example more than by our words, let us exhort people to do penance for their sins and to remember the divine commandments.[1]

An inner impulse sent them southward, to the end of what was then called the Plain of Spoleto, and then over the mountains. They continued to the Rieti Valley, for reasons that aren't entirely clear. What we do know is that the reception they received there was very different from Assisi. Francis would go on to have a long-term, affectionate relationship with the people there, and it likely began in 1208 or 1209 on a stop in Poggio Bustone, a hilltop town that clings to the lower reaches of Monte Rosato, high above the Rieti Valley. They set out an evangelical zeal, filled with the joy of their new mission.

The brothers customarily sought hospitality with the Benedictines, among whom they had some affinity. Above the town of Poggio Bostone was a convent, San Giacomo, and they were received there. Francis, who always loved mountainsides and cliffs, could not help but notice the dramatic cliff above the monastery and decided that he wanted to explore it. There were shepherds' paths in the mountains, but in this instance, he simply headed straight upward until he found a cave which he had heard about, one which would become one of his best-loved places. He wanted to be alone, to consider his future, but first he was tormented by his past.

He spent a day and a night there as he pondered the contradiction of God's call.

Why had God chosen him? He was deeply aware of his past sinful life. This was among the reasons that the people rejected him at home—they knew who he was. The memory of it ate away at him and caused him great doubt—even tempted him to abandon his call. He laid awake much of the night in torment.

Then something remarkable, even miraculous

happened to him. He realized that he was forgiven. That was it. Uncomplicated. God had forgiven him of his past life. He realized that the very essence of his vocation was that God chose him not *in spite* of his past life, but *because* of it. If Francis could be forgiven, could live a life for God, could not anyone? This realization was one of the greatest gifts of God's Spirit to him.

It felt as if a massive weight lifted from his soul. The jeers and taunts of his fellow townsmen in Assisi—the people who knew his past—no longer mattered. He was free, free to be loved by God and free to love others. Whenever he faced doubt in the future, he would come back to this moment, this revelation and take consolation in it.

But that revelation was not all. Freed from worry and the guilt of his past life, he fell into a deep sleep and in that sleep, he had a dream, a further vision from God in which he saw men and women by the thousands flocking to him. His small band of followers, in their freedom, love and poverty, would possess a charism that would be infectious. He awoke and turned the idea over in his mind: it seemed impossible, even preposterous to him, for they were only 12 at the time.

He descended the mountain as the sun rose, arriving at the convent. With excitement, he told his brothers of the revelation from God and, in his enthusiasm, went out into the center of the town, shouting to the townspeople *Buongiorno, Bene Gente,* "God Morning, Good People."

Thus began a special relationship with the people of

this valley that would remain until the end of his life, and which, in my experience continues to this day.

YOU CAN VISIT THIS "SACRO SPECO" referred to in English as the "Grotto of Revelation" when you stop in Poggio Bustone. There is a steep, well-marked path that leads above the convent of San Giacomo at the top of the town. It is approximately one kilometer long and switches its way back and forth as it leads past seven shrines. The path ends at a tiny two-story chapel that was constructed in the 14th century over the cave, below a sheer rock face that is held in place now by wire fencing. I have sat there for long times myself, and it's well worth pausing there for a time and reflecting on its importance in the life of Francis. A small porch at the upper level, just below the bell tower, has a pull rope and it is customary to ring the bell when you arrive, announcing to the valley below the good news of Francis's revelation over eight centuries ago.

7

Approval of the Pope

SINCE FRANCIS' small band came to number 12 souls, Bishop Guido, Francis's guardian in Assisi, felt that this small group needed the approval, and in a sense protection, of the Pope.

In the previous year, Francis had already sent his initial band of followers on mission, preaching to the people as they went. They had gone barefoot; he not only forbade them to accept money but to not even touch it. They were to serve others, particularly lepers and to beg their daily food. They were to accept the hospitality that was offered them, offering the greeting of "peace" whenever they entered a home. This was risky business in the early 13th century, as there were many independent and even dissident movements preaching throughout Europe who either opposed, or who appeared to oppose, the institutional church, in particular the clergy. It is important to understand that these crosscurrents, both political and religious, were dangerous and he needed to take care not to get caught in them. His genius was that he sought to reform the institution through the simple example of simply living Christ's original message, without directly challenging the institutional church.

Francis' lifestyle, in keeping with Jesus of the gospels —a lifestyle that was in sharp contrast to the material wealth and power of the Church—was intended more to persuade through love and grace, than through judgment. The approval of the Pope and his Curia, or ruling council, would provide protection and allow him and his small band to travel and preach freely.

They adopted the identity of "Penitents from Assisi" as they went and they used this term when they arrived in Rome in 1209, stopping to pray in the Church of St. John of Lateran, which was next door to the Lateran Palace (the home of the Pope) where they hoped to ask for an audience. They had friends in high places: Bishop Guido, who was there when they arrived, introduced them to several Cardinals and bishops, some of whom were drawn to Francis, eventually becoming his supporters over the next decade of his life. One of them, Cardinal San Paolo, listened over the course of several days and agreed to plead their case to the Pope himself.

It is important to understand that at this point in time the church had become a state itself, with all the temporal powers of any other kingdom. The Pope was like the king and his "cabinet" of advisors, the Curia, were the Cardinals, themselves drawn from the clergy, including bishops and archbishops. These prelates, or rulers of the church, were very much secular rulers, like princes. They owned property and enjoyed great privilege, and were often exempt from the control of local authorities, even raising and maintaining armies. Francis and his ragtag group of followers were essentially asking for an audience with the king and his court.

Pope Innocent III, himself inclined towards the poor, received the reports of Cardinal San Paolo and agreed to hear Francis. When Francis and his followers came before the Curia, barefoot and dressed in their simple brown habits, he spoke freely of their love of Jesus and the gospels and their intention to live a life of voluntary poverty and service. They only asked for permission to follow their inclinations; they didn't want to be forced to adopt another "rule" such as the Benedictine or Augustinian, which would have rooted or enclosed them. Francis and his small group wanted the freedom to move about freely and to have their own simple rule, which included poverty, chastity, obedience to God, humility, prayer, work, harmony and preaching.[1]

Innocent was moved, and he asked Francis and his men to wait outside. They had aroused conflicting responses from the Curia. Some, seeing their faith and simplicity, were stirred. Others, wanting to protect their wealth and power, thought them too dangerous and discouraged Innocent from granting them any approval to follow their life. Still others, thinking about other heretical preachers, were worried that they might arouse the people to oppose the institution of the church. Calling them back into the meeting, they were told that they would hear a decision about their request to follow their own rule in the following days.

The Pope, however, had another consideration: a disturbing dream he'd had some nights before. In that dream, he felt the Lateran Basilica trembling all around him, ready to collapse, but it was saved by a slight, young man who appeared and supported it on his shoulders; it occurred to him that Francis was *that* young man.

Days later Francis and the brothers were called back to the Curia and received the news that the Pope approved of them and their rule and would allow them to travel and preach freely. It is not clear if the Pope had any inkling of how many thousands of followers that Francis would have in the following years, but the friendship and support of the Pope and other influential leaders would come in handy in the years following, especially when the first woman, Clare, would come to join him.

Around this time Francis also insisted that his small band be known as the *Fratres Minores,* or "Brothers Minor" or "Friars Minor"[2] *Minore* was the term that was commonly used for those at the lowest level of society and Francis wanted his community to identify with and live among the lowest.

IN THE UPPER Church of St. Francis' Basilica there are 28 frescoes in a cycle of the Life of St. Francis and one of them shows Francis appearing before the Pope and another of Francis shouldering the collapsing Lateran Basilica. It is worth spending extra time there looking at these masterpieces, created by the famous Italian Gothic painter, Giotto, probably between 1296 and 1299. Besides being done within a century of Francis' life and death, they also visually tell what were then considered the most important stories and events of Francis' life, many of which I have attempted to share in this small book.

8

Conversion of Clare and her sister

IF THE CONVERSION of Francis and his companions was not enough for Assisi, the last straw came in 1212 with the arrival of the first woman to join their way of life: Clare di Favarone.

Clare, 11 or 12 years younger than Francis, came from a wealthy and influential family whose home was on the Piazza San Rufino, across from what would become the new cathedral of Assisi. Her father, Favarone di Offreduccio, was a knight; her mother came from an aristocratic family. When she was still young, her father died and Clare and her sisters had to flee with their uncle Monaldo (her father's brother) to Perugia after the family had caused trouble for the new commune. They would have been among the families that allied themselves with Perugia in the battle of Collestrada in which Francis was captured.

She returned to Assisi around 1207 after peace was struck between the commune and the dissident aristocratic families that had fled to Perugia. Having received an education during her time in Perugia, she would probably have been married within a few years to a young aristocrat, who would also receive a sizable dowry that her dead father had left her.

Instead, she came under the spell of Francis after she heard him preach. She adopted a simple dress and to the shock of her family, distributed her dowry to the poor, after turning down offers of marriage. Moved by his words, and likely more by his actions, she decided that she wanted to join him.

She told her intention to Bishop Guido, who was by now used to the many young people drawn to Francis. Francis soon became aware of her wishes, but before he could do anything he and Guido went to the Pope for guidance, who surprisingly gave his support.

On Palm Sunday, when all the young women of the city would come forward during mass to receive a sprig of olive leaves, Clare stayed in her place. When the bishop noticed that she had not come forward, he left the altar and brought one to her, signaling his support for what she was about to do. She was going to join Francis.

That night Clare left her fortified house under cover of darkness. Aided by some of Francis' followers, which probably included Rufino, her cousin, she made her way out of the city via the bishop's palace, where she would not be noticed. Along with Clare was her mother's cousin Pacifica, who would offer maternal protection. They made their way the three kilometers below the city to Santa Maria Degli Angeli. Francis knew she was coming.

Under the glow of torches, he asked her the questions and inquired about her obedience. She made her confession and took her vows before Silvester, the priest. As a sign of her commitment, they cut her hair. The brothers knew that at first light her family would discover her missing. To protect her, she was whisked away to San Paolo delle Abbadesse at Bastia, a benedictine convent just a few miles away.

In the morning, the family discovered that she was gone, and it immediately came out that she had gone to join Francis and his friars. Her uncle and cousins, armed and furious, rode down to the Porziuncola to bring her back, but found that she was not there. Finding that she had been removed to San Paolo, they rode there and attempted over the course of several days to persuade her to come back with them, but she refused. Finally, they resorted to force and broke into the sanctuary of the convent and found her at prayer in the chapel. As they rushed towards her, she stood and grabbed hold of the altar, symbolically an act of protection. As they attempted to pull her away, her head covering fell off and they saw that she had cut off her hair. Realizing that she was hopeless, they let her go.

Weeks later the scandal intensified when her sister Catherine also sneaked away to join her. This time Monaldo led a company of 12 men to attempt to rescue her, once again trying to entice her to return home. She refused. This time they were furious and, according to Clare's biographer, "… one of the knights threw himself at Catherine, slapping and kicking her. Then he seized her by the hair and dragged her off while the others pushed her and then tried to lift her in their arms." As they rushed between the brambles and bushes, her clothing was torn and tufts of her hair fell along the path. She called to Clare, who dropped to her knees in prayer. Then, the biography says, "Catherine's body immediately seemed to become so heavy that they couldn't lift her across the stream even when they were joined by men who had been working in the nearby vineyard—one of whom remarked that she must have been eating lead all night." They dropped her and Monaldo, furious, tried to beat her to death, "but when he raised his arm, such an excruciating pain shot through it that he couldn't."[1] He relented, and the family left them in peace.

Over the next months, Catherine also took her vows before Francis, alongside Pacifica. Bishop Guido gave San Damiano to the sisters, just a kilometer below his palace, where he literally and figuratively could keep a protective eye out for them.

Clare and her followers became known as the Second Order, eventually adopting the name the Poor Clares. Cultural customs of the time would have forbidden them to adopt a peripatetic life such as Francis', no matter how much they would have wanted it. Instead, they remained cloistered, committed still to the same life of poverty, where they dedicated themselves to prayer, to sewing and weaving, tending their garden, and working as much as they could on behalf of their poorest neighbors. Some of the brothers begged food on their behalf and left it outside the cloister, which was soon built for them to live in.

TODAY SAN DAMIANO remains much in appearance as it would have in the time of Clare and it is my favorite place in Assisi, still breathing the spirit of Francis and Clare.

When Clare died in 1253 a basilica was built in her honor at the southern end of the town, not far above San Damiano. It contains the original painted crucifix which spoke to Francis before he began the church's reconstruction. In the crypt of her Basilia, among other relics, you can see a lock of her light golden hair.

The Poor Clares, or Second Order, continues to this day. Four hundred years after Clare died, another woman entered the Order in Florence, Suor Maria Celeste, born Virginia Galilei, the oldest daughter of the famous scientist and astronomer, Galileo. As a scholar Galileo was discouraged from marrying the mother of his three children, so since Virginia was technically "illegitimate," Galileo sent her to be raised in the San Matteo Convent in Acreti, not far from Florence, where Galileo lived. At sixteen she joined the order, adopting her new name. She maintained a lifelong correspondence with her father, preserved in 120 letters. They reveal a woman with a bright mind (not unlike her father) who had a genuine interest in his work. Her name "Celeste" hints at this interest in her father's astronomical theories that, while true, were considered heretical at the time and which cost him dearly. The letters also reveal a deep affection that she had for him, and he for her. I recommend reading the beautiful book

Galileo's Daughter, by Dava Sobel, which chronicles her life from her letters, as well as her father's scientific insights and personal/spiritual struggles.

Galileo is buried in Florence, in Santa Croce, the world's largest—and perhaps most elaborate—Franciscan church. Because of the cloud over his reputation at the time he died, Galileo was originally buried in a side room. In the early 18th century, his remains were moved to a more elaborate tomb in the church's left aisle. During his exhumation remains of a woman were unexpectedly encountered; it is now accepted that they are those of Suor Maria Celeste, his beloved daughter, anonymously buried with her father. They were placed with his remains in his new tomb.

If you begin your pilgrimage in Florence, take the opportunity to spend an afternoon in Santa Croce.

PART II

The Character of Francis

9

The Wolf of Gubbio

THE LEGEND of how Francis tamed the wolf of Gubbio may be the best-known of the tales of the saint with animals. *The Little Flowers of Saint Francis,* a highly embellished 14th-century collection of these legends about Francis, tells it like this:

In the days when St. Francis abode in the city of Gubbio, a huge wolf, terrible and fierce, appeared in the neighborhood, and not only devoured animals but men also; in such wise that all citizens went in great fear of their lives, because ofttimes the wolf came close to the city. And when they went abroad, all men armed themselves as they were going forth to battle; and even so none who chanced on the wolf alone could defend himself; and at last it came to such a pass that for fear of this wolf no man durst leave the city walls.[1]

FRANCIS, out of compassion for the people of the city, found and then confronted the wolf. According to *Little Flowers* the wolf, teeth bared, "leapt toward Francis" but was stopped by Francis giving the sign of the cross. Addressing him as "Brother Wolf," Francis admonished the animal for having attacked and killed "both men and cattle" and for terrorizing the people. But then, rather than condemning him, he extracted from the creature a promise to change his ways and become peaceful. Francis, in turn, vowed that he would obtain a promise from the people that they would not try to take revenge for what the wolf had done. The wolf responded obediently, bowed his head, and "lifted his right paw and gently laid it in the hand of Francis, giving him thereby such token of good faith as he could." Immediately afterward, the wolf "set forth his side even as a pet lamb," as they walked side-by-side into the central square. In front of the marveling townspeople, Francis again obtained the promise from the wolf, who signified his acceptance in front of the town by bowing his head, wagging his tail, and offering his paw for a shake.

Thereafter, according to the legend, "Brother Wolf" no longer terrorized the townspeople but went peacefully from home to home where they fed him. He lived two more years before dying.

This legend is fascinating because of the way Francis played the "just" peacemaker, extracting a promise from the people of Gubbio to feed the wolf. This acknowledged that the wolf's behavior was due, in part, to his natural instinct to hunt for his food. In other words, the wolf also had needs, which Francis understood; this is why he didn't condemn him to death, or drive him away, as others might have done. Francis achieved not only a truce but *reconciliation* as an alternative to retribution.

As with any legend of Francis, its historicity is open to doubt. The story might be a conflation of several legends circulating at the time of Francis taming wolves in the mountain villages. Some historians speculate that the wolf may have been an outlawed lord of the countryside who terrorized the people. Whatever the source or origin—wolf or lord—the Franciscan historian André Vauchez, points to an even deeper significance in the story, concerning the roots of violence:

> Francis resolved the conflict by negotiating the wolf's right to reside in the town and, probably, to receive financial reimbursement since according to the legend the wolf was maintained to the end of his life at the expense of the commune. But whichever reading [wolf or lord] we give to this account its lesson is the same: between the human person and the animal, as in relationship between human beings, exclusion is at the origin of violence, whereas a fraternal and welcoming attitude makes its object aware of the joy of being included and prompts that individual to make peace.[2]

Francis, who had made service and care for lepers— the outcasts of society—a priority of his ministry, would have understood what it meant for any being to be an outcast. That gives the story, if not credibility, at least a deeper and lasting meaning.

Lastly, often overlooked in the hearing of this story is the miracle of the taming of the people, as Carlo Carretto points out. "The miracle of that morning in Gubbio was not the conversion of the wolf, it was the conversion of the people who lived in Gubbio—who for a fleeting instant believed it was possible to overcome a wolf armed only with food to give him instead of weapons to bloody him."[3] He sees other miracles at work here:

> What is extraordinary in the incident of the wolf of Gubbio is not that the wolf grew tame, but that the people of Gubbio grew tame—and that they ran to meet the cold and hungry wolf not with pruning knives and hatchets but with bread and hot porridge.
>
> Here is the miracle of love: to discover that all creation is one, flung out into space by a God who is a Father, and that if you present yourself to it as he does —unarmed and full of peace—creation will recognize you and meet you with a smile.[4]

THE STORY of the wolf comes to life as pilgrims walk the medieval streets of Gubbio. The old city walls are still intact, the wooded mountainside above them extremely steep, and one can imagine how they might have once felt dangerous. Near the top of the city, just below the old walls, is the tiny Chiesa di San Francesco della Pace, reconstructed in the 16th century over the purported cave of the wolf. Inside the crypt below is a medieval sarcophagus lid found nearby in 1873.

A sign says that the stone covered the bones of an animal—a veterinarian confirmed that they were the remains of a wolf.

10

Brothers at Montecasale

ABOVE THE CITY of Sansepolcro is an ancient convent of the Franciscans, Montecasale. It was originally a Benedictine Convent, founded in 1192, as a hermitage and hospice. In 1213 the Benedictines gave it to Francis, and he frequented it from then on. It clings to the edge of the mountain and has a dramatic view over the upper Tiber Valley, down toward Sansepolcro. It has two significant legends associated with it, both revealing different sides of Francis' character and what he wanted to model for his friars.

The first has to do with a band of three notorious robbers who lived in the vicinity. They were known to terrorize the locals who lived in fear of them. One day they came to the brothers living at Montecasale. They were hungry and begged food. But the brothers, knowing their reputation, refused to help them. They admonished them for their terror and thievery, sending them away in dishonor and shame.

Soon afterwards Saint Francis came to the sanctuary,

and the brothers reported proudly what they had done, presuming that Francis would approve, since they had reproved them for their sinful behavior. Instead of praising them, Franci rebuked them for their lack of hospitality. He knew what it was to be an "outlaw."

"Are they not humans, who are merely hungry? How can you refuse any one of God's children?"

Surprisingly, he instructed them, "Take some of the best bread and wine, go up into the mountains and call out for them. Take a cloth, set on it the feast, and beg forgiveness for your behavior." The brothers did as he instructed and with some reluctance the thieves came out of the wood, and while suspicious, ate eagerly. The brothers came back to Francis and told him what happened. "Well done," he said to them, "do it again." The next day they went again, this time gathering grapes, bread and wine, returning to the same place that they served the thieves. The thieves came out again, and with less suspicion ate eagerly.

The friars did it a third time, but by now the thieves were not at all suspicious of them, and greeted them warmly.

A few days later, the thieves, quite moved by the grace that had been shown them, came to the hermitage and spoke to Francis directly. They said that they regretted their lives and what they had done. They had heard of Francis and after meeting him in person, two of them decided that they wanted to join the brothers and took up the vows of the Friars Minor and remained with them until their deaths.

. . .

A SECOND LEGEND attached to Montecasale and teaches a different lesson.

In the early days of Francis, as his movement grew and his fame spread, many came to him and expressed that they wanted to follow him. Two such men came to him one day while he was in Montecasale.

Francis, who was a good judge of character sized up the two men, one of whom was a scholar and the other a simple peasant. Handing each a cabbage seedling, he instructed them to go into the garden and plant them. "Put them in the garden upside down, with their roots pointing upward." The simple peasant obeyed and went straightaway to the garden and did as Francis instructed. The second, the scholar, thinking the idea foolish, refused. "Everyone knows that you can't plant it with the roots upward. This is folly!"

He may have been correct, but for Francis it was not about the cabbage, but about the character of the man. He knew that a lot of what he asked of his friars was not logical, but needed to be obeyed anyway.

He praised the simple peasant, knowing that he might just be able to put up with the demands of following him.

But to the second, he replied, "You will not be fit for the order. There are things much more foolish that I may ask of you, things that you may find humiliating." So he left, disappointed, but Francis was relieved.

THE RELICS of the thieves remain to this day in the convent of Montecasale, which remains a Franciscan convent. In the lower chamber of the church you can find their relics (skulls, actually!) on display.

From Citerna, a hilltop to the west of Sansepolcro, and halfway to Citta di Castello, it is possible to take in most of the upper Tiber Valley, including Montecasale and Cerbaiolo (another Franciscan Sanctuary) as well as Monte Penne, the site of La Verna. A bit out of sight, but slightly to the south is the sanctuary of Buon Riposo. From this vantage point it is easy to see how Francis traversed this part of Italy, on the border of Umbria and Tuscany, with each sanctuary being about a day's walk from another.

11

Begged Bread is Holy Bread

FRANCIS REQUIRED his brothers to work; among them no one was to remain idle. Since he forbade them to touch money, they simply accepted food as payment. But if for some reason—such as being engaged in preaching—they were unable to work, then he commanded them to go begging. It was a practice he'd had his entire life as a poor brother and he embraced it with joy. He said, "Begged bread is holy bread. It is sanctified by the praise and the love of God. When a brother goes to beg alms, he first says, 'may the Lord be praised and blessed.' and then, 'give us alms for the love of the Lord God.'"[1]

However, in his time some brothers joined who were of high standing in the world and for whom begging was shameful. He impressed on them all the more that they should go and beg for their food. If they couldn't do it every day, then they should at least do it frequently, because if they became lax, they might again develop that old sense of shame rather than joy. He even felt that, "the more a brother had been noble and of high standing in the world, the more it would edify him and gladden him to go begging and do servile works for the giving of good example."[2]

As it one of his closest companions wrote,

… in the mind of Saint Francis begging almost for the love of the Lord God was a very noble, worthy and gentlemanly thing to do, both in the eyes of God and according to worldly judgment He reasoned that after mankind had fallen into sin, all the things that heavenly father had created for man's use were given to both worthy and unworthy men gratuitously as alms, because of his love for his beloved son. So, as Saint Francis used to say, a servant of God should beg alms for the love of the Lord more willingly and gladly than a courtly gentleman taking pleasure in his generosity. In making a purchase he says, 'give me this penny's worth of goods and I shall give you 100 pieces of silver for it.' The servant of God gives 1000 more than he receives because what he offers is the love of God and this is what a man gains in return for the alms he gives. Compared to God's love, all things on earth are as nothing—and even the things of heaven.[3]

Francis was often invited into the luxurious homes of the prelates of the church. They often sat at a well-set table with good food. One of his early supporters (and protectors) was the Bishop of Ostia, Ugolino, who would become the Pope Gregory IX. Once Francis was invited to a meal in the bishop's home (possibly in the environs of Rome) where several of his relatives and other Lords were present. Before the meal could begin, Francis slipped off secretly to go beg his food for the [= evening meal, as was his habit. He returned quietly and sat next to the bishop, which was his usual practice. Everyone saw his scraps of food and he even offered some of it to each of them. (Those who received his offering of food at a table considered it to be a relic and they cherished it for the rest of their life). The bishop was embarrassed, but hid his feelings until after the meal. Then, taking Francis into his bed chamber, he embraced him and asked him why it was he had embarrassed him so in front of his honored guests. Here was Francis's reply:

You, our Lord and ruler in the Pope's name, are ranked among the great and the rich in the eyes of the world. It is without doubt for the love of God that you and other exalted personages receive me into your houses, and even coerced me into coming. Nevertheless, when I'm staying in your house, I don't want to be ashamed to go and beg alms. Indeed I want to remain true to my belief that when I beg I do something very noble, and acting with royal dignity and honoring the all highest king who although Lord of all things, for our sake made himself the servant of all, and although rich and glorious and His Majesty, came among us in our humanity, poor and despised."

It is therefore my will to make known to those who are and will be my brothers that I consider it a greater joy of soul and body to sit at the poor table of the brothers, where I see before me the wretched alms they have begged from door to door for the love of the Lord God, and when I sit at your table, or at the table of other lords, set with food and abundance and variety and which is offered me in a spirit of reverence."[4]

It is said that Ugolino, astonished, blessed Francis for this, saying, "Do what you think best in the eyes of God and may the Lord be with you and you with him."[5]

12

Why You?

IN THE FIVE years after Francis and his friars received the support and protection of Pope Innocent III, the order steadily grew, with men coming from every level of society. One was a handsome, self-confident, and well-spoken young man named Masseo. Had he not chosen to join Francis, he could have become someone of influence, perhaps a burger or consul, or some other city leader. Masseo would become one of the best-known of Francis' followers.

Masseo, known as a solitary man of prayer, returned one day to the Porziuncola, perplexed by a persistent thought that came to him in his time of solitude. It was at a particular time when a steady stream of newcomers sought out Francis, so many that they strained to find places to sleep.

"Why you? Why you? Why you? Why is the whole world coming after you? You are not a handsome man; you are not learned or of great wisdom. You're not of noble birth. Why do they all come after you?"

Francis took little time to answer him, for he must have pondered this himself.

"I'll tell you why. It's because God could not find someone less qualified, or more of a sinner than me. It's because when God wants to perform his wonderful works, he chooses the weak and the absurd, those who count for nothing. That's why he chose me."

What Francis admitted about himself was true, and he struggled with the knowledge of his sinful past as long as he lived, as well as with his current shortcomings as the spiritual head of the Brothers Minor.

History does not record why Masseo asked the question—whether out of his own perplexity, or partly in jest —but he was so taken aback by the unexpected answer and by the profound truth that it revealed, that he became speechless, and some said, began an even deeper and more profound conversion that day. He became one of Francis' closest friends and along with Angelo, Leo and Rufino, was buried in Francis' tomb. He also lived the longest of any of them, dying in 1280, 54 years after Francis. He was probably at least 80 years old.

13

Francis preaches to the Sultan

IN 1213 FRANCIS had decided that he wanted to preach to (and hopefully convert) the Muslims (Saracens) in Spain. Recent Crusader victories had put more of the northern Iberian Peninsula under the control of Christian rulers. He wanted to convert the Saracens, rather than fight them with swords.

Francis and Bernardo took off for Spain, hoping to preach to the Arab caliph (Miramolino) He became frustrated when he found that the caliph had already retreated to Morocco. He and Bernardo waited in Barcelona for a ship, but Francis lost his voice and that was when they decided to head for Santiago de Compostela instead. We don't know much detail about this journey, but within a year there were apparently a dozen Franciscan sanctuaries in Spain. They were not the first friars to reach there; Giles and Bernardo had already been there 1208 already, and with pilgrims coming from all over Europe, the fame of the brothers was becoming known.

He and Bernardo returned to Italy, frustrated that he had been unable to preach to the Saracens. This was a long journey, over 5,000 km, at best taking most of a year. His mission was unfulfilled, but he continued the ambition, which evolved into a desire to convert Sultan al- Malik al-Kamil, who ruled over Palestine, Egypt and Syria.

WITH THIS IN MIND, in 1219 he went with five brothers to preach to the Crusade: Innocent had called for the Fifth Crusade at the end of the recent Lateran Council. The Crusades in some form had been going on for over 100 years. Their original purpose had been to free Jerusalem for pilgrimage, but there was also a certain apocalyptic drive; since the year 1,000 had passed, some thought that Jesus' second coming might come about with the occupation of Jerusalem under Christian control. The First Crusade achieved its goals, but in the subsequent century nearly all of what they gained was lost, mostly due to squabbles among themselves.

Francis intended to reach the Crusaders who were then in Egypt, attempting to wrest control of it from the Sultan. For the crusaders, there was a sense that the whole world had to be converted by whatever method, including the sword. Francis' hope was to convert by example, rather than by force.

He had a letter of introduction from Pope Honorius III. It took six weeks to cross to Damietta. That spring, before he left, he had (with difficulty) rebuffed Ugolino and many within his own movement that pressed him to either accept one of the existing Rules (Benedictine, Augustinian) or write one of his own. He was gradually developing a sense that the control of his own movement was slipping. This might explain why some early biographers were convinced that he traveled in search of martyrdom.

When he arrived, he found the behavior of the so-called Christian armies shocked him, with murder, drunkenness and sexual license. In subsequent battles they proved heartless and ruthless, and Francis was appalled at their bloodthirsty methods. He had seen battle nearly two decades earlier, but this was worse than anything he had known. As he pondered how to proceed, he nursed the wounded.

Sultan al- Malik al-Kamil was an educated, genuinely devout man who wanted to avoid bloodshed. He was the same age as Francis, equally committed to his faith, and very pious, outwardly.

On repeated occasions he offered generous terms to end the conflict, including giving the Crusaders control again of Jerusalem, which had been their goal all along. Pelagius, the papal prelate was much greedier (as were merchants from Italy and elsewhere) and imagined that they could not only regain Jerusalem, but control all of the Middle East, if they would just hold out. The result were numerous battles and sieges that caused the unconscionable massacres of tens of thousands.

. . .

IN THE MIDST of the horror and bloodshed came Francis, and what happened next was, according to Franciscan biographer Don Spoto, "...unprecedented in the history of Muslim-Christian relations."[1]

Accompanied by Illuminato, one of the brothers who knew Arabic, Francis approached the Sultan's lines under a flag of truce. He asked to speak to the Sultan, and surprisingly, his soldiers allowed this, probably seeing from their dress that they were some sort of "holy men." They led him to Malik al-Kamil.

In this unusual audience with the Sultan, Francis preached to him about Christianity, in an attempt to convert him. His manner was audacious, but humble, and the Sultan was impressed, but also perplexed about what to do with this man.

The Sultan considered the advice of his chief religious counselors—that Francis should be executed for trying to convert a Muslim to Christianity—but apparently the Sultan saw something in Francis's genuine and simple faith, his manner, dress, and spirit and it moved him enough that he not only spared Francis, but allowed him to stay for days while being engaged in a dialog about their respective faiths. They parted with a mutual respect for each other, with Francis able to return safely to the Christian lines. In the end, Francis succeeded neither in converting the Sultan, nor in achieving martyrdom, but he did win a friend. The Sultan, as they parted, also gave Francis free passage to Jerusalem, a journey he likely undertook, though he did not speak of it.

Francis, unfortunately also failed to end the bloodshed, but he accomplished one thing: creating an example that long has outlived the confused and sordid history of those times.

THE SULTAN SENT gifts along with Francis, including a silver horn that today is visible in the Lower Church in the Basilica.

PART III

Francis' Last Years

14

The forming of the Tertiaries

FRANCIS HAD CREATED A FAIRLY austere rule for his friars (the First Order), which the Pope had modified for the Poor Clares (the Second Order). Yet Francis was aware that many others were attracted to him and his way of life, people who were already married and would be unable to take on the vow of chastity. They might also have children or other relatives to provide for. Such folk were attracted to his fraternity from its earliest days on and, in Franciscan fashion, he had kept a loose association with these people for nearly a decade. They were formally established in 1221 as the Third Order, or *Tertiaries*, an order of people who would live in the world, keep marital or familial commitments, but live as much as possible in imitation of the life that Francis himself lived.

One of the best-known to us in history was Giacoma de Settesoli, a noblewoman of Rome. Born in 1190, she was younger than Francis and already had two sons by the time she made her acquaintance with Francis, when he and his friars came to Rome in 1209 for their audience with the Pope. Legends say that she sought spiritual advice from him then and he advised her to live a life of charity and simplicity, which she did. Her husband Graziano, opposed to the papacy, still had a long-running lawsuit with the Pope when he died 1217. As a widow Giacoma became one of the wealthiest women in Italy and she intended to use her wealth to assist Francis. He stayed at her home whenever he visited Rome. She obtained for him and his friars the chapel and hospice of San Biagio, where Francis stayed in 1219 when he visited Rome. On this place in 1231 the Franciscans built the church San Francesco a Ripa.

It is said that he gave her a lamb which he had rescued from the slaughter, which she kept as a pet, and that she used the wool sheared from this sheep to make his burial shroud.

Giacoma remained close to Francis for the remainder of his life and was one of the few women allowed into the quarters of the friars. She was such a common fixture among them that she earned the nickname "Brother Jacoba." She would later be one of those in attendance when he died. (See chapter 21) After the formal acceptance of the Third Order, she moved to Assisi and remained there until her death in Feb. 1239. Proof of her high esteem was the fact that her remains are interred in the crypt near St. Francis, along with the four brothers who were closest him.

When she joined the Third Order (some say Francis founded the Third Order thinking of her) she dropped her lawsuit against the Pope, and that might be a reason the pope so enthusiastically supported the founding of the Third Order.

While we don't know what she looked like there is a Simone Martini fresco in the transept of the lower church of St. Francis' Basilica which is thought by many to represent Clare, but there are those who think it is actually Giacoma de Settesoli. Around her head are seven suns in a halo – *sette soli*. And Clare is ordinarily shown in a religious habit, including in other works by Martini in the Basilica.

The Rule of The Third Order was approved in 1221. Called "Penitents," the members of Third Order also followed a simple life of service, a life of prayer, all in the context of marriage or family, living "in the world" alongside their fellow townspeople. One critical commitment was not to take up lethal weapons or make oaths. This curbed the power of local lords, who had the power to raise armies from among their subjects.

IN THE COURSE of the following centuries many people from all classes of society joined the Third Order and some prominent figures were purported to be members, including (possibly) Michelangelo and a number of popes.

Among the earliest was Queen Elizabeth of Hungary, wed to Ludwig prince of Thuringia, in Germany, who was a devoted and loving husband. Already a devout woman, when she met Franciscan missionaries, she became more committed to serving the poor, contributing to them from the wealth of her royal fortunes. After the death of her husband, she joined the Third Order. She died young, at age 24, in 1231, just five years after Francis. She was buried in the church in Marburg and canonized just three years later.

A half century later, her great-niece, Elizabeth of Portugal became famous for her peacemaking efforts between her unfaithful and profligate husband, King Denis of Portugal and their son, Alfonso. She later helped avert a war between Castile and Portugal. She established hospitals, orphanages and religious houses throughout her kingdom. After her husband died in 1324, she made a pilgrimage to Santiago and took on the habit of a Franciscan Tertiary. She retired to a life of personal poverty at a monastery in Coimbra, where she lived the last 11 years of her life, until her death in 1336. Known as (and later canonized as) the "Peacemaker" she emerged from her solitude on numerous occasions to intercede between rival monarchs.

Closer both in time and geography to Francis was Angela of Foligno. Born in 1248, she was from a wealthy background. She lost her mother, her husband and her three children during an outbreak of the plague. She had already been influenced by the preaching of a Franciscan, Brother Arnold, and felt moved to give up her wealth and privilege and enter into a life of prayer and service to the poor after a pilgrimage to Assisi. Known for her mystical experiences and writings, she eventually gathered around her a community of tertiaries, women and men, living lives of humility, poverty, charity and peace, and for whom she served as spiritual mother. She died in 1309.

Recent centuries also produced people who imitated Francis, while not being part of any of his orders. One of those is Carlo Carretto, an Italian, born in 1910, who joined The Little Brothers of Jesus in the Moroccan desert, a community founded by Charles de Foucauld. Known as a prolific writer of spiritual books, he left the Little Brothers after a decade and returned to Italy where he lived eventually in an experimental lay community in Spello, in the former Franciscan convent of San Girolamo. Besides his book, *Letters from the Desert*, he also penned *I, Francis* a book that Robert Ellsberg called, "… a personal diagnosis of the church and the world delivered in the 'voice' of Francis."[1] Written in the first person, in the persona of Francis, it is hopeful and engaging. I find the book has some of the best modern, spiritual insights into the message and the meaning of the life of Francis.

EACH OF THE two Elizabeth's burial places was a destination of pilgrimage in the Middle Ages, and modern marked pilgrimage routes exist to Marburg (and connecting to Santiago.) Coimbra, the burial place of Elizabeth of Portugal, is on the Camino Portuguese.

Saint Angela is buried in the Franciscan Church in Foligno, about a quarter kilometer from the entrance to the city, along the Way of St. Francis.

You can visit the community of San Giralamo (and the burial place) of Carlo Carretto a short walk north of Spello.

15

Fonte Colombo and the Rule of 1223

DURING FRANCIS' time in Egypt, it had been rumored that he had died. The friars as well as the leaders of the church were relieved when he returned alive to Italy in the fall of 1220.

By then Francis, it could be said, had become a victim of his own success. The recent chapters, or meetings of brothers, had been attended by thousands. Through preaching and mission work the brothers had established themselves throughout Europe. Respect towards them grew, and priests and scholars had come to join him and with this came the temptation to own houses and collect books. Francis, always wary of property and the learning that came from books, tried through example and dictates to suppress this, but it would not happen. He had seen that the ownership of property required the force of arms (which he forbade his friars) and the temptation to become cloistered, no longer living among the people. Author Don Spoto said, in reference to the monasteries, that Francis saw that with property, "… wealth brought power, power diluted the presence of the gospel. Bishop Guido, after all, owned half the real estate of Assisi and he spent most of his time in litigation and little in the care of his people."[1]

In contrast to other radical reform movements, Francis had the protection of the church. Spoto said further,

> …because he had no grandiose plans to revolutionize or even reform the church, there's no evidence for heresy or insubordination that could be brought against him. He wished to change only the world's moral and spiritual perspective, primarily through the gentlest and most unobtrusive example, and through identification with all societies outcasts. As opposed to the fixed regulations and rhythms of the monastery, Francis had something both freer and more difficult in mind: flexibility of the gospel and the initiative of men of goodwill on the alert for the promptings of the spirit rather than the letter of the law.[2]

To those who ruled the church, the friars represented an opportunity to reform the institution; to others they were a counterweight to the influence of more severe reformers who broke with Rome. The friars had pledged obedience to Rome and were thus a model. Some scholars and priests saw the acceptance and preference as an opportunity for their own advancement, not the purest of reasons.

Francis, who was better at inspiring than organizing,

had always avoided a written rule; it was not his nature. He said over and over that his Rule was nothing more than what the Gospels taught and he wished that his movement could retain that simplicity. Still, after the acceptance of the order in 1215, he had been urged to write one, which he finally consented to do in 1221. It was simple, mostly references to the passages from the Gospels, a slightly expanded version of the informal Rule that won the approval of Innocent III in 1209. Presented to the Chapter, or gathering of friars, it caused a stir. Elias, now the head of the order, had rejected it as too severe and he was supported by other prelates and clerics and by the authorities of the church.

The friars also believed that the Rule of 1221 did not have enough punitive measures. For example, Francis allowed that anyone who had taken a vow of chastity, and broke it, to simply be put out of the brotherhood, but not condemned to hell or anything. They were not allowed to ride horses, for only the wealthy could own horses and Francis forbade the ownership of books or houses. From the point of view of the authorities and many of the new brothers who were clerics, this made it difficult to have a stable life.

Retreating to Fonte Colombo in 1223, he revised his rule of 1221, making it much shorter and eventually gaining acceptance by the Roman Church. But while he felt he had made too many concessions, had also surrendered his will and accepted whatever came next. However imperfect he felt it may have been, it allowed his followers protection of the church, not unlike the way he had accepted the bishop's cloak decades before.

FONTE COLOMBO IS a different sort of Sanctuary for Francis. It's existence as a Benedictine convent from the Abbey of Farfa, preceded him by centuries. It is about a five kilometer walk from Rieti and Francis had come here often, the monks of Farfa having given it to Francis and his brothers for their use. He gave it the name Fonte Colombo after seeing a small flock of doves watering in the spring just below the convent. The small and simple Chapel of Mary Magdalene was there already and inside there is a red "tau" on the window sill which legend ascribes to Francis. The whole place sits on an escarpment looking over the Rieti Valley, with its back-drop of mountains to the east.

Francis had often come there and discovered a cleft in the rock just below the chapel where he liked to go to pray and above it his friars eventually constructed another small chapel, dedicated to St. Michael. Though it is now covered over with glass, you can still see the steps that they cut into the rock, down to the cave of Francis.

You can see a copy of the Rule of 1223 on the wall in the church.

16

Greccio and the first nativity -
Francis and animals

THE STORIES of Francis and animals are legion, from the tale of preaching to the birds at Canara, to the singing locust who lived near his cell at the Porziuncola, to the taming of the wolf at Gubbio. That a human of kind and patient nature—especially non-threatening—might be able to communicate at a deeper level with animals is documented and known throughout history and cultures.

But the story of the first live Nativity scene staged at Greccio at Christmas in 1223 is deeper than that. Its date and the context may tell us much more.

In the fall of 1223, Francis having already written his final Rule, was still in the Rieti Valley. Francis, who left us few writings, found more power in symbolic actions—staging scenes or performances—the stuff of legends, which spoke more loudly than words on paper. As Christmas approached, Francis was beginning to turn his final thoughts towards the future, the future of his Order and his own future. I wonder if at a deeper level he was sensing that his end was not too far away. Having written his revised order, he was now free from the burden of the demands of governing.

He decided to create a dramatic event which would combine his love and devotion to animals with his love of people. He was fond of the people of Greccio, simple farmers who had accepted him since he had come to receive the hermitage, originally a cave in the mountain. Many of them became members of his Third Order.

Thus, it was natural that Francis combined his need to model the simplicity of his order, his love of creation and his wish to point to the humanity of Christ and the miracle of the incarnation by re-creating the original nativity. Greccio was given to him by Giovanni di Velita, a local lord who later became a member of his Third Order. In Francis' time it consisted of little more than a cave and small simple wooden huts.

He asked the local farmers and shepherds to all come together on Christmas Eve and meet him at the cave, where he had a doll in the manger to represent Christ and some simple townsfolk to represent Mary and Joseph. They brought their own animals, who stood around the scene, as they may have during the original birth of Christ. They arrived by torchlight and Francis recounted to them the story of the nativity in great celebration. It was a powerful event, symbolizing an emphasis to living by the Gospels, not a "Rule." Francis preached, recalling how Jesus had been born in poverty and powerlessness, worshiped and adored by the simple and poor.

Recent scholars say that he might have had even

more in mind, thinking back to his talk with the Sultan and a subsequent visit to Jerusalem. Aware that the crusades had been launched in order to rule over the original Jerusalem, they speculate that by staging the Nativity, he was signaling that the incarnation happens anywhere. Christians did not need to possess the Holy Land; they did not need to shed so much blood. Thus, Greccio could become the new Bethlehem, freed from the constraints of time and place.

He was not completely done yet with the Rieti Valley, but this event at Greccio could be seen as a gift of Francis to the local community, his parting gift.

GRECCIO, like Fonte Colombo, is along a variant of the Way of St. Francis. It can be reached by foot (though it's a day's walk) or by train, stopping at Greccio Station and climbing about 4 kilometers along a pleasant country road.

17

The mystery of the Stigmata
at La Verna

WITH ITS LEGENDS and dramatic setting, La Verna blends together all the inspiration, mystery, and contradictions of Saint Francis. He had chosen a life of total poverty, dedicating his energy to preaching and serving the poor, but he didn't stop there. He was hard on his body, performing frequent long fasts and enduring cold and extreme weather, often clothed in little more than his tunic. He often gave away the very cloak that kept him warm, and he slept directly on the ground or on rock.

He was so hard on himself that in the last years of his life he was perpetually ailing, which curtailed his ministry. Exactly why he chose to be this way is open to speculation. His biographers, both medieval and modern, suggest that it was in penance for his licentious past and as an example to others in a world of ostentatious wealth and power. He also had a frail body to begin with, and his imprisonment in Perugia as a younger man may have left him with lifelong illnesses, such as malaria. In stories about their lives, saints always appear to be hard on their bodies, which seems to be a requirement, their stories often embellished to the point that it is difficult to distinguish between fact and exaggeration. This was the case with Francis, though there is no doubt that enough of it was true; he admitted toward the end of his life that he had been too hard on his own "Brother Body."

Francis at this point in his life had withdrawn almost completely from the community; he was part, but not a leader. His new Rule went away from his original intentions of poverty and while he kept those himself, to the end, he retreated as often as possible to the hermitages. Thus we find him at La Verna in Sept. 2025. He was often just in the company of his closest brothers, Masseo, Leo, Angelo and Rufino.

He had begun coming to La Verna after it came to him in 2013, when he met the Count of Chiusi, Orlando Catani, at a feast. The Count was so moved by Francis' preaching and the witness of his way of life that he told him about La Verna. He said,

> I have in the Tuscan region a most venerable mountain called mount of La Verna which is very solitary and wild and is extremely well adapted to anyone wants to do penance in a remote place from people, or who wants to lead a solitary life. If it is pleasing to you, I will willingly give it to you and to your companions for the salvation of my soul.

The place, interestingly, had a long history, dating

back to the times of the Romans, and before. It was they who gave it the name, dedicating it to the Goddess La Verna, the patron saint of thieves. In Francis' time it was known to still harbor thieves and if you approach it from the west, you will come through a magical beech forest, with its jumble of boulders, where it is easy to imagine thieves hiding. The sanctuary itself sits dramatically atop an 80-foot cliff along the side of Monte Penna. Monte Penna has a unique profile, looking like a man with a crew cut. It is visible from as far away as the Consuma pass, above the Arno river, to the Northwest, to Citerna in the upper Tiber valley, 60 kilometers to the south.

Francis had already suffered the loss of everything dear, more than a decade earlier. Next he had to suffer the loss of what was dearer to him—his brotherhood. He had been their model, their symbol, their mentor... Now, by suffering the wounds of Christ he was experiencing an even greater loss—just as Jesus had experienced it, through the greatest of bodily suffering in crucifixion. Francis, who had wanted to be as like Jesus as he could, would now have those marks.

THE STIGMATA supposedly appeared on Francis during the 40-day fast ending at Michaelmas (Sept. 29) in 1224, two years before his death. He received five wounds— one on each hand and foot and one on his side—similar to the wounds of Christ. This is likely the first recorded instance of this in history. They were reportedly painful and debilitating, but he hid them under bandages, and they were reportedly not seen until after his death when a number of witnesses attested to them. Clare was one of the few who witnessed them in his lifetime, and she made a pair of slippers to cover his feet.

Ever since the first reports of them—a few years after his death—they have been a subject of skepticism and controversy. Some modern biographers are dubious about the divine origin of these wounds, suggesting that they were the result of some other disease or illness, and many doubting that they occurred at all. Yet his later medieval biographers were not in doubt, nor are many of the million faithful who come here each year to visit.

He would only live two more years from the time that he received them.

AT THE SANCTUARY of Laverna one can visit a chapel which was built over the site where Francis prayed and received the imprint of the stigmata. The Franciscan community has been processing daily to the Chapel of the Stigmata for nearly 600 years, a testimony to the centrality of Laverna—and the stigmata—to the witness of St. Francis.

Visitors should also take time to descend to the Sasso Speco or sacred "jutting" rock that forms a natural roof over a deep cleft. It was apparently a favorite place of Francis' and may have been a feature that drew him originally to the place.

18

The Kinship of All Creation:
The Canticle of the Sun

AFTER FRANCIS RECEIVED the stigmata at La Verna, he returned to the environs of Assisi. He wished to go to the Porziuncola, but seeing him so unwell, Clare insisted that he stay at San Damiano, where she and her sisters could care for him. Since the sisters were cloistered, and allowed very limited contact with men (even Francis) a small hut was constructed in the garden outside the convent for him.

At this point in his life, Francis was suffering physically: his stomach ailments were ever-present, he was nearly blind, and his wounds from the stigmata continually bled. It was perhaps during this time that Clare sewed for him the slippers which he wore over his feet, to conceal the wounds there.

Of all his ailments, Francis seemed to suffer most with his eyes. It was so bad that he couldn't bear the daylight, not even the firelight, and he lay suffering in the darkness. If that were not enough, according to the *Legends*[1], he was plagued continually by the mice, who jumped on his table, nibbled at his food and ran across his body as he tried to sleep on a simple woven cot, so much that he was unable to sleep. He considered their presence a trial from the devil.

One night, in his torment, in self-pity, he cried out to God in a lament, and it is said that the Spirit then spoke to him:

> Suppose someone were to give you a recompense for these illnesses and tribulations of yours. It would be a treasure so great and precious that if all the earth were pure gold, all the stones precious stones, and all the water balm, you would even so look upon all these materials as nothing, and esteem them as worth no more than mere earth, stones, and water in comparison with the great and precious treasure being given you. Wouldn't that make you happy?

Francis replied that it would indeed be a great treasure to strive for. The Spirit then spoke further, telling him to be jubilant and joyful in all his illnesses and tribulations, saying that he could be, "...as sure of having it as if you were already in my Kingdom."[2]

The next morning his demeanor was different, and he told his companions of the message and the assurance that it gave him of being destined for God's Kingdom. In joy he composed the first verses of his "Praise of the Lord for His Creatures," which began with a praise, "All-highest, good Lord...," but eventually came to call it the Canticle of the Sun, because he praised "Brother Sun" first, and later praises Sister Moon, the stars, Brother Wind, Sister Water and so on. It expresses his kinship with all of the great manifestations of nature.

What strikes me, as I read them, is how simple this hymn of thanks is. The shine of the moon, the light of the sun, the refreshing splash of water, the sound and cooling touch of the breezes—these are all free. Like everything else of Francis, he celebrated the abundance that God freely gives and which we must not hoard.

He asked brother Pacificus, known to be a master singer in royal courts, to help him to set it to music and then asked him to select other musical brothers, to travel throughout the country singing this great song of praise to the people.

The great consolation he received through this revelation and the composition of his Canticle sustained him through the last painful years of his life.

He soon added more verses, one to Brother Fire, another to reconciliation and forgiveness and a final one to Sister Death, as will be told.

19

Miracle of the grapes at La Foresta

IN THE LAST years of his life Francis was in great physical and spiritual torment. Slight of build, never physically robust, he suffered from numerous illnesses in his life. He may have picked up tuberculosis when imprisoned in Perugia, or malaria when he traveled to Egypt to preach to the Crusaders and the Sultan. The wounds in his hands and feet (the Stigmata) were excruciatingly painful.

His eyes, the organs through which he beheld his beautiful world, became diseased as well, possibly with trachoma, a disease spread by flies, possibly picked up in Egypt. The disease painfully swelled the underside of his eyelids.[1]

Consequently, light became unbearable to him. He, who had written the beautiful Canticle of the Sun, could no longer bear its brightness. He spent more time in his beloved caves, partly out of a need for darkness. Pus continually oozed from his eyes.

Through his contact with bishops and Cardinals and

significant clerics, he was told of a prominent doctor, Tabuldan the Saracen, who was known to treat eye diseases. He had a treatment for this which consisted of cauterizing the veins in the temples. (The very idea of it makes me cringe.)

While waiting for his treatment (which would occur at Fonte Colombo) he traveled in the fall of 1223 to the Rieti Valley where his following was great and among whom he was revered and deeply beloved. Looking for a quiet place to rest, he sought refuge at the country church of La Fabian, about five kilometers from Rieti. Francis had come to the Rieti valley frequently; his history with the people stretched back 15 years to when he and his first brothers traveled there and found a spiritual openness that was the diametric opposite of Assisi. He had a small cell underneath the church, where he stayed for some weeks.

This small country church was served by a poor priest who maintained himself on the income of a small vineyard. He harvested about twelve bags of grapes per year, which when turned into wine could be exchanged for wheat, hemp and other foods and necessities.

News of Francis' arrival at the small church spread quickly in the city and in the countryside and many flocked to see him, to hear him preach and to have him lay his hand on their children in the form of a blessing. In spite of wanting solitude, he didn't have the heart to turn the people away.

The crowds sat on the grass outside the church to hear him preach and when they were hungry wandered up and down the rows of the vineyard, which was laden with bunches of purple, ripe grapes. They helped themselves generously and by the time the crowds were gone, the vineyard was nearly stripped bare. Francis, who saw this happen, made no effort to stop the people.

This provoked the anger of the priest, who watched helplessly as his annual income vanished before his eyes. He rebuked Francis in front of the brothers and accused him of impoverishing him. Francis understood his anguish, but cautioned him to not worry—was he not a servant of the God, of Jesus, who had told him to "not worry about life, about what to wear or what to eat?"

When the people were gone, Francis told the priest to go through the vineyard and gather up what few remaining clusters he could find, and he did this, putting them into the vat where they could be trodden for making the "must" for wine. He promised the priest that when all was done, he should have 20 measures of wine; if it was less, he would make up for the difference himself. The priest obeyed him and gathered in the remaining harvest, trod it out for the vintage.

And no one knew how it happened, but later when they measured out the wine it amounted to 20 measures. The priest, in amazement came to believe in God's providence for his needs and said that even if the whole vineyard had been left intact, it could never have produced 20 measures of wine.

FRANCIS EVENTUALLY RECEIVED the treatment for his eyes that was prescribed by the bishops, in Fonte Colombo in 1215. The prescribed treatment for the pus in his eyes was to cauterize the veins in his temples, believing that this would stop the pus from oozing in his eyes. The doctor took a poker in the fire until it was red hot and then placed it on Francis's temples, drawing a line between the top of his ears and the outside corner of his eyes. It was more than most of the brothers could bear to be present for this, but it is said that Francis felt nothing. Unfortunately, the procedure was a failure

It is said that after this he after this he added a verse to his canticle, a hymn to brother fire.[2]

> All praise be yours, my Lord, through Brother Fire,
> through whom you brighten up the night.
> How beautiful is he, how playful!
> Full of power and strength.

YOU CAN VISIT the church and sanctuary of La Foresta, though you will need to make an appointment because the church and attached building is a home to a drug treatment program. Today the little house is intact, with its stone tank for the must, as is the cave where Francis slept. It is one of the few sanctuaries of Francis that is not up on a height; nevertheless, the place exudes the peace and solitude of his other sanctuaries.

PART IV

Francis Makes His Final Journey

20

Home to Assisi

IN THE YEAR after he received treatment for his eyes, Francis' health, already poor, declined even more. The wounds on his side, hands and feet oozed blood. In Assisi, Clare had made him slippers to cover his feet, but even so he had trouble walking. His eyesight was nearly gone after the failed operation.

Hopeful that his health could still improve, the brothers took him to the sanctuary at Cortona, but it was to no avail. Unable to walk, he was carried on horseback and taken to Bagnara, in the mountains to the east of Assisi, hoping again that his health would improve. Instead, it declined further. Knowing that the end of his life was near, Francis wanted to go home to his beloved Porziuncola. Fearful that armed men from Perugia would try and snatch him, so that he could die there (so that they could raise his basilica and house his relics) he was escorted, ironically, by armed knights. I imagine an emaciated man, weighing less than 100 pounds, strapped to the front or back of a knight on horseback, too weak to refuse his armed escort.

When they arrived in Assisi, they were offered hospitality just outside of the town. The knights accompanying him went into the city and tried to buy food, but were refused. They went back to Francis and asked him for something, but he admonished them:

> I'll tell you why you couldn't find anything: you trusted your flies (he meant their money) and were not trusting in God. Now go back to the houses where you tried to buy food and see to it that you are not ashamed this time. Ask the people to give you alms for the love of God. The Holy Spirit will inspire them, and you will get what you want, and plenty of it.
>
> So, they went and begged alms as the Holy Father had told them to do, and the men and women very cheerfully and very generously shared with them what they had. The soldiers came back happy and joyful to Saint Francis and told them what had happened. In their opinion this was a true miracle because they had seen verified to the letter what the Holy Father had foretold.[1]

The entourage stopped in Assisi on their way to the Porziuncola. Francis had heard that the mayor and the bishop were fighting with one another. It got so bad that the bishop had excommunicated the mayor and the mayor forbade anyone to do business with the bishop. The entire town suffered in the conflict and in order to bring peace, Francis added another verse to his *Canticle of the Creatures*:

> All praise be yours, my Lord, through those
> who grant pardon for love of you;
> through those who endure sickness and trial.
> Happy are those who endure in peace, by you,
> Most High, they will be crowned.

He had the mayor summoned to the bishop's residence where one of the brothers sang the verse to them both. Moved by the words and by the suffering of their friend Francis, they made peace with one another.

The entourage left Assisi and continued down the slopes of Mount Subasio until they reached the Porziuncola and Saint Mary of the Angels, first stopping at San Damiano so that he could say farewell to Clare and the sisters. It was in the garden of San Damiano that he first wrote the *Canticle of the Creatures* and now in the presence of the sisters, he wrote the final verse:

> All praise be yours, my Lord, through Sister Death,
> from whom no one among the living can escape.
> Woe to those who die in mortal sin!
> Happy those She find doing your will!
> The second death can do no harm to them.

His final wish was now fulfilled: he had arrived at his beloved Porziuncola, to die.

21

The Death of Francis

FRANCIS SPENT his last days with his closest brothers, Leo, Ruffino, Masseo and Angelo, who had been looking after his physical and spiritual needs for several years. Knowing he was about to die, he wanted to bestow a special blessing upon Bernardo, the first brother who had joined him. Bernardo came into the room and sat next to Giles, another of the earliest brothers. Francis, blind, reached out his hand to lay it on Bernardo's head, but instead touched Giles. Though he could not see, his sense of touch was still keen and he recognized his mistake. Bernardo moved closer and Francis gave him special blessing:

> The first brother the Lord gave me was brother Bernardo, and he was the first one to undertake and fulfill in all perfection the perfection of the Holy Gospel by giving away all his goods to the poor. For this reason and in consideration of many other prerogatives, I have

greater love for him than for any other brother in the whole Order. Wherefore I will and ordain, insofar as it is in my power, that whoever the minister general may be, he should love him as if he were me. And may the provincial ministers and the brothers of the whole order look upon him as my proxy.[1]

Bernardo indeed received special honor for the rest of his life, and in blessing Bernardo I see Francis affirming for all who witnessed it the simple beginnings of his community.

Francis then asked for someone to write a letter for him to Jacoba, requesting that she bring some special almond cakes that he had always loved and some of his favorite cloth to make a tunic for his burial. But before the brothers could dispatch the letter to her in Rome, they heard the approach of horses and Giacoma appeared at the door with both the almond cakes and the cloth. She would be the only woman allowed to be present in the room as he died.

In his last hours, as his end approached, he asked them one last favor: to strip him of his clothes and lay him naked on the earth as soon as he drew his last breath. *Il Poverello*, the Little Poor Man, the one who loved the earth, the stones, the dirt, the birds, the flowers —in short, everything—this man wanted to come back into contact with that earth. The man who courted Lady Poverty, the one who was in love with God, who was eager to love everyone with whom he came into contact—this man wanted to return symbolically and literally to the earth. He loved the soil, and so he returned to it.

Lying there naked, he was once again—as he had been decades before up the hill in the courtyard of the bishop's palace, standing before the crowd—stripped of his clothes, completely free. At that very moment, a flight of larks—his favorite—took wing above the small chapel.

22

Francis' Final Resting Place

ALL OF ASSISI heard of his death, and the throngs poured down to the little chapel in the woods to pay their last respects. When his body had lain naked on the earth, all those present were able to witness the stigmata on his body.

His body was laid in a simple casket and transported on foot up to Assisi. The friars stopped first at San Damiano, where they lifted the lid and allowed the sisters to touch his body as they wept in their grief. They then carried him the last kilometer up the hill to the edge of the city, where he was buried in the crypt of San Giorgio, his home parish, not far from the courtyard of the bishop where he had originally stripped off his clothes and began a life of poverty. The prophet turned out to be honored in his hometown.*

Elias, who had been for a time the Governor

---

* San Giorgio is now longer there; it was torn down a few decades later to make way for the Basilica of Santa Chiara.

General of the Order under Francis, was a controversial figure. While he was gifted in organizing in the way that Francis was not; he lacked the charism of Francis. Still, along with the new Pope Gregory IX, the former Bishop of Ostia, the former Ugolino—Francis' advocate and friend—he planned and raised funds for a magnificent Basilica to be constructed in his honor, two churches, one above the other. Land was donated about a kilometer below the walls of the town, a place called "Hells Hill" because it was where the city gallows were located. Francis had once said that he would like to be buried there, a place that looks over the Valley of Umbria, the landscape and people that he loved, though towards the end of his life had stated that he wanted to be buried at the Porziuncola.

MEANWHILE, reports of miraculous cures began to circulate about those who were healed at his tomb. Normally it would be long process of gathering testimony, conducting interviews and carrying out investigations—perhaps taking many years—before someone could be canonized. Such was the deep love and honor for Francis, and the abundance of stories of miracles, that he was canonized in record time, on July 26, 1228, less than two years after his death. The very next day they laid the cornerstone of the Basilica. In 1230 the lower church was complete, and Francis' body was transferred from San Giorgio to the crypt. There was a great deal of controversy surrounding the moving of his body. The "translation" or moving of a saints' remains was often said to be accompanied by miracles. Crowds would have pressed around the casket, convinced that touching it, or even his body, would heal them and there was even fear that the masses might dismember the corpse or take a scrap from his burial clothing, but his body arrived unscathed and was entombed directly below the altar. Construction continued on the upper church, and it was finally consecrated in 1253.

His resting place became a place of pilgrimage, as was Santa Maria degli Angeli in the valley below Assisi. An enormous basilica—among the world's largest—was later raised over the humble Porziuncola in the 16th century and it dwarfs the tiny chapel that Francis so loved.

THE BASILICA OF ST. Francis soon became one of the most-visited pilgrimage sites in Italy, though it is not clear how easy or common it was for laypeople to go down into the crypt and pray at his tomb. Within a little more than two centuries even that became impossible: another war had raged between Assisi and Perugia and when the latter's forces pillaged the town in the 15th century, Pope Sixtu IV had the passageway to the tomb sealed and hidden and it remained lost for nearly another four centuries. Located again in 1818, the crypt was remodeled and open to laypeople, with a further reconstruction again in the 20th century.

The crypt itself is a peaceful place to visit and all pilgrims who go to Assisi should go there. Beside the tomb of Francis, I find it especially moving to note that at the four corners of the chamber are buried the four close companions of his last years:

    Ruffino d. 1249

    Angelo d. 1258

    Leo d. 1271

    Masseo d. 1280

EQUALLY MOVING IS an entombment located at the stairway coming down into the crypt. It reads:

    Jacoba dei Settosoli

    Nobildonna romana

    Devotissima a San Francisco

    d.1239

"A noblewoman of Rome, very devoted to Saint Francis." She was originally buried in the church above, but her remains were moved to this spot in 1932.

The Canticle Of The Creatures

Most high, all powerful, all good, Lord!
all praise is yours, all glory, all honor, and all blessing.
To you alone, Most High, do they belong,
and no mortal lips are worthy to pronounce your name.

All praise be yours, my Lord,
through all that you have made,
and first my lord Brother Sun, who brings the day;
and light you give to use through him.
How beautiful is he, how radiant in all his splendor!
Of you, Most High, he bears the likeness.

All praise be yours, my Lord,
through Sister Moon and Stars;
in the heavens you have made them,
bright and precious and fair.

All praise be yours, my Lord,
through Brothers Wind and Air,

and fair and stormy, all the weather's moods,
by which you cherish all that you have made.

All praise be yours, my Lord, through Sister Water,
so useful, lowly, precious and pure.

All praise be yours, my Lord, through Brother Fire,
through whom you brighten up the night.
How beautiful is he, how playful!
Full of power and strength.

All praise be yours, my Lord,
through Sister Earth, our mother,
who feeds us in her sovereignty and produces
various fruits with colored flowers and herbs.

All praise be yours, my Lord, through those
who grant pardon for love of you;
through those who endure sickness and trial.
Happy are those who endure in peace, by you,
Most High, they will be crowned.

All praise be yours, my Lord, through Sister Death,
from whom no one among the living can escape.
Woe to those who die in mortal sin!
Happy those She find doing your will!
The second death can do no harm to them.

Praise and bless my Lord and give him thanks,
And serve him with great humility.

Timeline of Francis and Clare of Assisi

Some dates are approximate

1181-82? Francis Born in Assisi

1194? Clare born in Assisi

1197-8 Civil War and expulsion of nobles; "commune" proclaimed in Assisi; Rocca destroyed; city walls rebuilt

1202 War with Perugia; Battle of Collestrada; Francis' capture and imprisonment

1203-4 Francis' long sickness; period of malaise and wandering

1204-5 Second attempt at being a knight; falls sick in Spoleto and returns home

1206 At San Damiano Francis hears message to "rebuild my church"

1206-7 Break with family and adopts hermit's habit; travels to Gubbio

1208 Rebuilds San Damiano; first brothers join him; poverty to be their vocation.

1208 Brothers fan out on mission; Francis receives revelation in Poggio Bustone

1209 Twelve brothers travel to Rome; Pope blesses (but does not formally recognize) the new order

1210 Brothers develop St. Mary of the Angels as headquarters on Benedictine land; this becomes known as the Porziuncola

1212. Clare leaves family on Palm Sunday; forms new order, Poor Clares

1213 Count Orlando gives La Verna to the Franciscans

1215 Francis travels to Spain with Giles in an attempt to reach Morocco; instead goes to Santiago de Compostela. There are already 14 Franciscan houses in Spain before he arrived there

1215 Full recognition of Francis' order at the Lateran Council

1217 General "chapter" of brothers, with thousands in attendance

1219-2 Francis Travels to Egypt; Preaches to both Christian Crusaders and to the Sultan

1221 Writes first Rule, which is not accepted by the Vatican

1223 Writes second Rule at Fonte Colombo, which is accepted by the Pope

1223 Live Christmas Nativity at Greccio

1224 Receives Stigmata at La Verna during Fast of St. Michael in September

1224 Composes *Canticle of the Sun*, first poem in Italian; travels to Rieti for eye surgery; stays at San Fabiano and performs the miracle of the grapes

1226 Dies on the evening of Oct. 3-4

1228 Francis proclaimed a Saint; Work commences on his Basilica

1230 Consecration of Basilica of St. Francis and relocation of his remains to the crypt

1253? Clare dies

1256 Clare proclaimed a saint

1258 Clare's Basilica started

1260 Completion of St. Clare's basilica

Notes

Introduction

1. Rohr, Richard, "A Prime Attractor," daily meditations, May 17, 2015, https://cac.org/daily-meditations/a-prime-attractor-2017-06-05.
2. Ibid
3. Seracchioli, Angela Maria, *On The Road With Saint Francis*, p. 4
4. Ibid, p. 5

4. Cheerful builder

1. House, Adrian. *Francis: A Revolutionary Life*, p. 77. This quote from House seems to be originally from the *Legends of the Three Companions*.

6. Good morning, Good People

1. *Legends of the Three Companions*

7. Approval of the Pope

1. This summary is drawn from *Francis of Assisi: A Revolutionary Life*, by Adrian House, p.87.
2. Ibid, p. 105.

8. Conversion of Clare and her sister

1. The sources of this part of the saga come from the *Life of Clare*, author unknown, but possibly Thomas of Celano, quoted in *Francis of Assisi: A Revolutionary Life* Adrian House, pp. 132-134.

9. The Wolf of Gubbio

1. Author unknown, *Little Flowers of Saint Francis*, pp. 34-5.
2. Vauchez, Andre, *The Life and Afterlife of a Medieval Saint*, p. 276.
3. Carlo Carretto, *I, Francis*, p. 92
4. *Ibid*, p.86

11. Begged Bread is Holy Bread

1. *We Were With Francis*, p. 11.
2. Ibid.
3. Ibid., p. 7.
4. Ibid., pp 10-11
5. Ibid., p. 11.

13. Francis preaches to the Sultan

1. Spoto, Donald, *Reluctant Saint: The Life of Francis of Assisi* p. 161

14. The forming of the Tertiaries

1. Ellsberg, Robert, *All Saints: Daily reflections on Saints, Prophets and Witnesses for Our Time*, p. 149

15. Fonte Colombo and the Rule of 1223

1. Spoto p. 171.
2. Ibid p. 165

18. The Kinship of All Creation: The Canticle of the Sun

1. See *We Were With Francis*, pp, 166-172
2. We Were With Him, p. 168-9

19. Miracle of the grapes at La Foresta

1. House, Adrian, *Francis: A Revolutionary Life*, p. 214.
2. See Appendix for the *Canticle of the Creatures*

20. Home to Assisi

1. *We Were With St. Francis,* p.6.

21. The Death of Francis

1. *We Were There,* p.54

Bibliography

Butlere, Salvator OFM, translator, *We Were With St. Francis.* Assisi: Edizione, Porziuncola, 2008. This book is a collection of stories from Angelo, Ruffino and Leo, three of St. Francis' closest companions, translated from a medieval manuscript called the *Legends of Perugia.*

Brown, Sandy, *Trekking the Way of St. Francis: From Florence to Assisi and Rome.* Milnthorpe, Cicerone: 2015.

Carretto, Carlo, *I Francis.* Maryknoll, Orbis, 2022.

Cetolini, Rodolfo, *The Sanctuary of La Verna.* Rimini: Pazzini Stampini Editore, 2003.

Eanes, Russ, *Pilgrim Paths to Assisi: 300 Miles on the Way of St. Francis.* Harrisonburg: The Waker Press, 2023.

Francke, Linda Bird, *On the Road with Francis of Assisi: A Timeless Journey Through Umbria and Tuscany, and Beyond.* New York: Random House, 2005.

Fusarelli, Brother Massimo, *The Franciscan Sanctuaries of the Rieti Valley.* Genova: B. N. Marconi, 1999.

Giandomenico, Nicola, *Art and History: Assisi.* Florence: World Publisher

Harms, Matthew, *The Way of St. Francis.* Harrisonburg, Village to Village Press, 2023

House, Adrian, *Francis of Assisi: A Revolutionary Life.* Mahwah: Hidden Springs, 2001.

Rohr, Richard, *Eager to Love:* The Alternative Way of Francis of Assisi. Cincinnati: Franciscan Media, 2014.

Seracchioli, Angela Maria, *On the Road with Saint Francis.* Milan: Terre de mezzo, 2004. Translated by Leaslie Ray.

Spoto, Donald, *Reluctant Saint: The Life of Francis of Assisi.* New York: Penguin Compass, 2002.

Vauchez, Andre, *Francis of Assisi: The Life and Afterlife of a Medieval Saint.* New Haven: Yale University Press, 2012. Translated by Michael F. Cusato

Index of places that go with the stories

LOCANDA GUIDI
di Veri Simona s.a.s.
Via Luca Pacioli, 46 · Tel. 0575 741907
52037 Sansepolcro (AR)
Part. IVA e Cod. Fisc. 0169762051 2
19/4/22

CAMMINI DI SAN FRANCESCO
SANSEPOLCRO
19/4/22

HOTEL LE MURA
CITTA DI CASTELLO
Via Borgo Peruse
Tel. 075/8521870
Fax 075/8521350
20/4/22

LA VIA di ROMA
LA VIA FRANCIGENA di SAN FRANCESCO
CITTA' DI CASTELLO
20/4/22

MARKET
ORTALI
PIETRALUNGA
21/4/22

B&B
di Valle
Fraz. Loreto, 27 Tel. 347 9768879
Cod. Fisc. SNT NLS 49P59 L551U
22/4/22

DIOCESI DI GUBBIO
Parrocchia di
CENTENARIO DELLA
23/4/22

DIOCESI DI GUBBIO
CE
Chiesa Eggubina
ISTITUTO MAESTRE PIE FILIPPINI
23/4/22

Chiesa di
San Francesco
della Pace
Gubbio
24/4/22

Fratello Lupo
Chiesa Arcosale
24/4/22

25/4/22

26/4/22

Acknowledgments

I want to thank Sandy Brown, guidebook author, who invited me o tell these stories on a tour of his. Afterwards he suggested that I write them down, and so now we have this book.

I also want to thank my wife Jane, who has accompanied me on most of my pilgrim journeys, and who is my first and best editor and critic. I couldn't have done it without you.

I thank also the many pilgrims who have been with me on the Way of St. Francis, or on one of the several Caminos de Santiago and who have give me the motivation to keep learning and sharing about what we learn from pilgrimage. That community, scattered across the world, has been the great gift of my later years.

Also by Russ Eanes

PILGRIM PATHS *to*
ASSISI

300 MILES *on the*
WAY OF SAINT FRANCIS
———
RUSS EANES

This is the story of a pilgrimage to Assisi on the Way of St. Francis—several pilgrimages actually: three on foot and one inward of the spirit. The journeys on foot took six weeks, over the course of several years; the inward one—to be inspired and even transformed by the life of Francis of Assisi—began decades ago and continues today, as all inner journeys should.

The outward journey to Assisi began in 2018 in Santiago de Compostela in northwestern Spain as I entered the crowded western plaza outside the legendary cathedral. I had just completed a 500-mile pilgrimage on foot. Walking the Camino de Santiago was the culmination of a dream that had bubbled along in my life for 20 years. In that journey I had joined my steps with the millions who had walked before me. It was a walk through space, time, and history.

That pilgrimage was life-changing, and I knew that I wanted to do something like this every year for as long as I lived. I had started that walk solo, but my wife, Jane, joined me during the last week. We entered the plaza together that day—a day I still regard as one of the most significant of my life. We decided that we would take another pilgrimage, this time in Italy along the Way of St. Francis, but first I needed to complete my book about walking the Camino de Santiago. Over decades, we had been moved by reading about the life of Francis, even naming our second son after him. We always planned one day visit Assisi, his birthplace and home.

(From the Introduction to *Pilgrim Paths to Assisi*)

The WALK of a LIFETIME

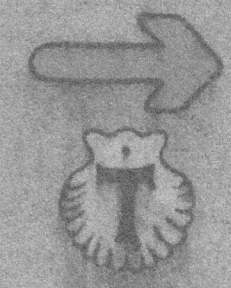

500 MILES *on the* CAMINO DE SANTIAGO

———

RUSS EANES

Foreword by Arthur Boers

Praise for The Walk of a Lifetime

Books on the pilgrimage to Santiago de Compostela are many, but few capture the richness of the experience as well as Russ Eanes' *The Walk of a Lifetime*. It merits a slow reading so that it's spiritual and human truths might be deeply savored. Russ shares not just details of his walk along the Camino de Santiago in Spain, but the grace that carried him forward and left its mark on his heart forever. —Kevin Codd, author of *To the Field of Stars: A Pilgrim's Journey to Santiago de Compostela.*

Reading his book was like getting to walk the Camino all over again…Some Camino memoirs make you wish that you had had the opportunity to walk alongside the author. Eanes' is one of those… Walking with him was an absolute delight.
–Roni Jackson-Kerr, reviewed in March 2020 *La Concha*, quarterly newsletter of the American Pilgrims on the Camino

Reading Russ Eanes' *The Walk of a Lifetime* was the next best thing to doing the entire Camino. I felt like I was walking with him every step of the way. If you can, do the Camino. If you can't (at least this year), read the book.
—David Brubaker, Dean Eastern Mennonite University

About the Author

Russ Eanes is a writer, walker and cyclist from Harrisonburg, in the lovely Shenandoah Valley of Virginia, where he lives with his wife Jane, three of his adult children and five of his eight grandchildren. He loves to lead hikes in the nearby Blue Ridge ad Allegheny mountains. He also enjoys traveling, gardening, reading and photography. In 2018 he "downshifted" to experience a less hectic pace of life and is now writing books, and teaching older adults about "Slow Travel." He also leads biking tours around the U.S. and walking and hiking tours in Europe, including the Way of St. Francis.

This is third book.

For photos and more information about his books or tours, to go RussEanes.com

www.ingramcontent.com/pod-product-compliance
Lightning Source LLC
Chambersburg PA
CBHW070339130626
46556CB00007B/2945